Modernizing Women

Modernizing Women

Searching Their Identities

KALI NATH JHA

RAWAT PUBLICATIONS

Jaipur • New Delhi • Bangalore • Mumbai

ISBN 81-7033-954-5

Published by
Prem Rawat for *Rawat Publications*
Satyam Apts., Sector 3, Jawahar Nagar, Jaipur 302 004 (India)
Phone: 0141 265 1748 / 7006 Fax: 0141 265 1748
E-mail: info@rawatbooks.com
Website: www.rawatbooks.com

Delhi Office
4858/24, Ansari Road, Daryaganj, New Delhi 110 002
Phone: 011-23263290

Also at Bangalore and Mumbai

Typeset by Rawat Computers, Jaipur
Printed at Chaman Enterprises, New Delhi

Dedicated
to the memory of
my wife
MANJU

Contents

Foreword

Modernizing Women: Searching Their Identities by Dr. Kali Nath Jha is a commendable addition to the studies on the problem of women in search of identities in a region of Bihar. He offers an empirical perspective on this problem in the backdrop of the processes of modernization. Extensive sociological literature is available on the theme how identities are generated or rekindled in the process of modernization. This study is an addition in this context. It deals with the formation and change in women's identities and deserves our attention.

The study is based on a survey of 200 highly educated women from Darbhanga district of Bihar. Dr. Jha has adopted the method of stratified random sampling, and data have been collected using a 'schedule'. Attitudinal changes among women in response to questions on issues related to 'identity' and 'change' constitute the basic frame of reference for his study. Analysis has been done keeping in view existing sociological works relevant to this theme.

The book is a timely addition to a very relevant aspect of women's study in India. I hope it will be widely received by readers and researchers.

Yogendra Singh
Emeritus Professor
Centre for the Study of Social Systems
Jawaharlal Nehru University
New Delhi - 110 067

Preface

"The process of modernization is accretive, assimilative and adaptive. It occasionally threatens established social order. Modernization, unlike social movements, constitutes a process of social, political, cultural and economic transformation which by its nature tends to be accumulative and adaptive, and which selectively promotes structural replacements and differentiation in society".

In the traditional society, women were confined to household affairs and according to traditional and religious sanctions it was obligatory on their part to serve their father in the pre-marital period, the husband after marriage and the sons in the latter part of life. Outdoor activities were beyond the jurisdiction of Indian women. They were not allowed to participate in politics and economic affairs of the family. But in the present age, women are participating in outdoor activities like men. The discrimination on the basis of sex has been eliminated with the concept of equality of the two sexes being widely propagated and honoured.

This study is a systematic investigation into the indices of modernity found in the community life in Darbhanga district of Bihar. It is concerned with highly educated women, who represent the progressive section of womanhood and display the emancipation of Indian women.

I wish to express my profound gratitude to my guru Yogendra Singh, Emeritus Professor of Sociology, JNU, New Delhi, for providing me guidance and encouragement to complete this work. I owe him much for his kind consent to write a Foreword for the book.

I wish to express my sincere gratitude to Prof. K.L. Sharma, Vice-Chancellor, Rajasthan University, Jaipur, Prof. Abha Avasthi (Lucknow), Prof. Anand Kumar (JNU, New Delhi), Prof. Amrit Srinivasan (IIT, New Delhi) and Sushila Jain (Jaipur) for their encouragement and inspiration in the completion of this study.

My sincere gratitude is due to Soumendra Patnaik (Delhi), Rajesh Mishra (Lucknow), Nilika Mehrotra (Delhi), Sukant Chaudhary (Lucknow), Lalit K. Mehta (Jaipur) and Manju Sinha (Principal, Ranchi Women's College, Ranchi) for their help and encouragement in completing this study.

I am thankful to Susmita Dasgupta (Delhi), Ruchi Ramesh (Simla), Gaurang Sahay (TISS, Mumbai), V. Sujatha (Goa), Kiran Preet Kaur (Chandigarh), Reema Bhatia (Miranda House, New Delhi), Sabiha (CWDS, New Delhi) and Lakshmi Bhatia (Sahay), New Delhi for their scholarly comments on this work.

I cannot forget my friend Vinita (Singh), Ranchi Women's College, Ranchi, who has encouraged me and has provided shelter and support and, often, more direct inputs for this book, either through guidance towards relevant materials and references or by helping me to work out my arguments through discussions.

I am grateful to Urmilla Singh, Ajay Singh and Jai Palak for their affection and encouragement. I am also grateful to Suresh Mishra, Kishori Mishra and my brothers Bishwa Nath Jha and Kailash Nath Jha for their affection.

My little ones—Madhu and Abhas, who supported me considerably during the course of my study, deserve my best blessings. My wife passed away before the manuscript of this book could reach the stage of publication. In Rowena Robinson's words—'if heaven is and has an address, she's sure to order a copy'.

I thank Rawats, who are always pleasant, efficient and wonderful to work with. The anonymous reviewer of the manuscript provided several useful suggestions.

Kali Nath Jha

1

Introduction

The term 'modernization' is commonly used in everyday life. Generally, modernization refers to the acceptance of modern tools and equipments, and becoming westernized in dress style and overt behaviour. Modernization is not only a change in the material culture of a group or the material position of an individual but it is also concerned with a change in the belief system and the ideological framework. Modernization refers to change in overt behaviour, in the outlook, mind set and thought process. Modernization is a process which brings much desired, value orientation, motivations and norms. It is a process of transformation of a society from its backward framework to a forward looking, progressing and prospering structural build up. It started with the colonial history of many nations. It is true that after Second World War, it has been speeded up and has become broad-based.[1] Modernization does not take place only at the superficial level. A society may adopt scientific inventions and yet remain in the twelfth century with respect to its ways of thought and belief. Such a society will still be underdeveloped. A villager who sits in a train or watches television but keeps his women in 'purdah' is not a member of a modernized society. We can say that his orientation is taking place but unless he accepts a scientific outlook, he is a liability in a progressive nation. Modernization is neither the process of imitation nor of adoption though it includes both. In reality, it is a process of changing of the outlook of man.[2] An individual enjoying all the material comforts of the modern age may not be called modernized if he is faith-oriented in outlook and tradition-dominated in his approach. On the other hand, a person deprived of modern material comforts may be called 'modern' if his orientation is scientific and outlook, rational. Modernization is a process of change in outlook from being traditional and religious to being rational.

The process of modernization involves an interaction between the existing ideology and the necessary ideological framework that is required for development and progress according to one's ideology. Modernization is a complex process involving the denial of 'some' things of the past and the acceptance of some 'new' things. Thus, there exists a contradiction between the 'old' and the 'new'.

The process of modernization demands the full utilization of scientific discoveries, inventions, technological developments and available natural resources. It focuses on the social and economic development of a society on a rational basis. A modern society may accept those values of cultural heritage which are not outmoded. At the same time, a modern society accepts new values which are equated with the political and social ideology of the society and then the specific patterns of modernity are defined as per that society. Thus, (all) societies of the world do not have identical concepts of modernization.

Modernization is scientifically examined and analyzed by Yogendra Singh and we follow the same line. Modernization is a universally accepted model and has a relevance to ideology. But certain attributes of modernization are universal. In this context, it may be treated as a kind of 'cultural universal'. The universal attributes of modernization are pan-humanistic, trans-ethnic and non-ideological. Singh explains that "modernization approximates to such a cultural order. It symbolizes a rational attitude towards issues, and their evaluation from a universalistic and not particularistic viewpoint; when it involves an emotional response to problems, orientation is empathic and not constrictive; modernization is rooted in a scientific worldview; it has a deep and positive association with levels of diffusion of scientific knowledge, technological skill and technological resources in a particular society. But what may be essential to modernization is the commitment to scientific worldview, the internalization of humanistic and philosophical viewpoint of science on contemporary problems and not merely the volume of technological advancement. It is possible that a society as also a person might command a maximum of scientific skills and resources but a minimum of its necessary psychic and emotional requisites. It is otherwise possible that a successful scientist may be a failure as a *modern* human, and a most affluent or technologically advanced society may also be one which is most tyrannical. It is in this context that the meaning of modernization should be understood. And it is in the context of meaning that we could distinguish the changes implied by modernization from other forms of cultural changes that orthogenetic civilizations have undergone in contact with exogenous cultural systems."[3]

The distinction between modern values and traditional values may be maintained on the ground that modern values, like science, being evolutionary universal, might not be typical to any one particular cultural tradition, whereas traditional cultural values may be particularistic and typical. It may be purely accidental that institutions contributing to modernity first developed in a culture other than one's own. Modernization in its essential attributes or in ideal-typical forms is a universal-cultural phenomenon. Like science, modernity is not an exclusive possession of any one ethnic or cultural group, but belongs to humanity as a whole. This, however, should not mean that in all substantive details all modernized societies or cultures will be alike. On the contrary, the existential adaptations to modernization in every society, as evidence suggests, take a historical and distinctive form. But the substantive adaptation to modernization should be distinguished from modernization *per se* since in all likelihood, not for a long time to come (perhaps never), anywhere in the world shall we have a fully modern society.[4]

On the question of rationality, Yogendra Singh writes: "The focus on the pre-eminence of the role of rationality dominates most discourse on modernity. The analytical categories that we have used in this context, such as 'myth', 'history' and 'reason', are critical to our comprehensive analysis of this discourse. As widely accepted by sociologists, modernity implies a measure of 'disenchantment' with tradition. Tradition is supposed to be embedded in the 'enchantment' ideology about the life-world. Enchantment implies faith in the formulation that the normative principles governing life-ways in all of their aspects of manifestation have been 'revealed' by the Divine. It cherishes the faith that their origin is in the 'sources' that could not be challenged on the basis of utilitarian rationality as championed by science and technology. Historically, these are associated with the Enlightenment ideology. Even if we accept the Weberian explanation that in Europe the rise of rational capitalism, democracy and the social institutions based on rational legal authority owe their origin to the Protestant reforms introduced by Calvin, the fact remains that Weber also accepts that the nature of this rationality was governed by the reformation values which exhorted commitment to a moral order and personal ethic of conduct (anchored on the responsibility to the Divine according to that work was defined as 'calling', motivating the followers to perpetual self-less labour to make this world 'kingdom of God on earth') which gave rise to industrial capitalism. However, as soon as the mantle of the church was removed from this ethical foundation of rationality, the revolution of the industrial capitalism in Europe and elsewhere turned into an 'iron cage' bereft of moral sensibilities, being guided entirely by the profit motive and ruthlessness of the utilitarian goals.

The question, however, remains as to whether the cultural sphere of our life, which reaches into the frontiers of economy, polity and social institutions, does indeed tend to be defined entirely by the utilitarian rational principles? Is there no scope in our rationalization or critical appreciation of our life-world and our social institutions for the application of normative or evaluative principles based on the supra-rational values? Also, to what extent does the history and collective memory of a people influence the manner in which they evaluate innovations in cultural, economic and social life? The contemporary discussions dealing with the discourse on modernity (including those which deal with economic, political and social-cultural globalization) increasingly recognize that the initial historical conditions as well as the universal and pervasive urge among people to legitimize their identity through celebration and re-invention of tradition enhances the significance of the supra-rational ways of defining normative issues. The role of myth and the mythic mode of normative legitimation is, therefore, continually revived and celebrated.

The mythic sources for the search of identity and legitimation gain ground also because the scientific paradigm of rationality and utilitarianism fail to resolve several crucial problems of the human condition which constitute the enigma of contemporary life in the 'modern' world. It is noticed that scientific reason not only explains but also mystifies reality. The solutions that science offers, on which the discourse of modernity largely rests, are not only revisable but often misleading. These have failed to resolve the issues which continue to bedevil the ideology of universal humanism and human rights. The asymmetries of power, exploitation of the weak by the strong, the continued social and cultural discriminations of people based on birth, gender, ethnicity, religion and nationality etc., have not ceased with the modernization of our life-world. These, and several other aspects of the contemporary processes of modernization, globalization and universalization of cultural and economic institutions, are therefore, perceived by people not entirely through a 'scientific rational' prism. The scope for the mythic legitimation and rationalization of the cultural processes continues to enjoy validity in the ambience of ethical uncertainty and ambiguity which the contemporary processes of globalization of culture have generated."[5]

According to Yogendra Singh, "social movements aim at collective mobilization to bring about changes in the social structure that may be reformative or revolutionary, but they have one feature in common, that is, the discontinuous and historical nature of their lifecycle. This distinguishes the process of social change brought about through movements from the process of change through modernization. The latter, though anchored in an ideology or a normative system, constitutes a process of more or less steady role and status differentiations necessitating, in course of time, a basic re-structuration of society. Generally, the process of modernization is accretive, assimilative and adaptive. It occasionally threatens established social order causing what Eisenstadt calls 'breakdown' in the social system (mainly triggering revolutionary movements or political authoritarianism of various kinds), because of the grossly uneven nature of growth in the social structure, causing inequalities among different social strata (Eisenstadt, 1964) or resulting from the lack of equilibrium among the contradictory social forces released in society during the process of modernization and their mis-management. Otherwise, modernization, unlike social movements, constitutes a process of social, political, cultural and economic transformation which by its very nature tends to be accumulative, adaptive and which selectively promotes structural replacements and differentiation in society. Since modernization is a multidimensional and ideological process it gave rise to a great deal of debate in India during the 1960s and 1970s (see Singh, 1973, 1978; Kothari, 1970a, b; Dube, 1973; Srinivas, 1966; Singer, 1972). In this debate, not only were the issues of cultural adaptation or synthesis raised, but the discussion also focused on whether the *traditional* social institutions, structures and beliefs in India would be able to assimilate the roles, structures and values required for *modernization*. The empirical observations were, however, unanimous that traditional institutions, beliefs and social structure responded positively to the demands of modernization. They underwent selective adaptive changes in order to accommodate the requirements of modernization. The observations differed on the nature and the degree of unevenness of opportunities available to various castes, communities and groups to benefit from modernization, or the extent to which modernization sharpened the awareness of this unevenness of social, economic and cultural inequalities in society."[6]

There are two key concepts, viz., 'social structure' and 'tradition', which have been used by Yogendra Singh to analyse the forces of modernization. Singh writes: "The systems of 'social structure' and 'tradition' cover the entire gamut of the Indian social phenomena and its realities. Modernization in this system begins either from the emergent and endogenous sources or through contact with forces outside the systems."[7]

Education and Modernization

Contemporary education, which is an agent of modernization in various forms, is also of western origin. Traditionally, content of education was esoteric and metaphysical; its communication was limited to upper classes or the 'twice-born' castes and the structure of its professional organization was hereditary and closed. The roles both of the teachers and the taught were qualitative-ascriptive. Modern education has a fundamentally different orientation and organization. Its content is liberal and exoteric and it is steeped in a modern scientific worldview. Freedom, equality, humanism and denial of faith in dogmas are the themes which a modern education should contain. It has a professional structure which is not ascribed to any specific group or class but can be achieved by merit by any one in society. Some branches of modern education such as science, engineering and medicine directly focus on a worldview which embodies the core values of modernization, and imparts skill to realize the goal of a modern society. Traditional Indian education departed fundamentally from these normative and organizational prerequisites.

The foundation of modern education in India was established by the British. Its historical landmarks are: Macaulay's policy of 1835 to promote European learning through English, Sir Charles Wood's dispatch of 1854 which for the first time recognized the need for mass education with private and missionary help and gave up the policy of selective education known as the 'filtration theory', and finally the first Indian Education Commission of 1882 which recommended the initiative of private Indian agencies in the expansion of education.[8]

Yogendra Singh has analysed the significance of education in the process of modernization. Singh writes: "From the very beginning a contradiction between the primary and the college-university level of education emerged in India on account of the medium and content of education. At the primary level, the medium of instruction (with the exception of missionary and public schools) was the regional language and at the college level it was English. Teaching of science and European literature was done at the colleges and universities to which a select few had access; but the mass education at the primary level remained isolated from this main current. This lag in the structure of education which started from the time of Macaulay has still not been fully bridged. Modernization through education thus, right from the beginning in India, has been confined to a sub-culture of college and university educated youth and elite and never did become a mass phenomenon."[9]

In the nineteenth century the rush for higher education, specially among the urban middle class and the growth in higher education was also considerable.[10] Yogendra Singh explains that "the significance of education in modernization could be analysed in three areas: first, the cultural content of this education, secondly, its organizational structure and thirdly, the rate of its growth. The content of new education was doubtlessly modernizing and liberal in nature. This is true whether reference is made to the humanities or social science or natural and applied sciences. The literary content of the courses in the humanities and social sciences was drawn from the literature of the European Renaissance, Reformation and Enlightenment. Its themes were humanistic, secular and liberal. For example, "John Stuart Mill's essay 'On liberty' soon after its publication became a text in Indian colleges. Indians came to know about Magna Carta, and the struggle for liberty and equality in Europe and America. The implications of modern science became manifest in their studies" (Tangri, 1960-61). An important element in this education was emphasis on contemporaneity and humanistic evaluation of social, political and historical issues. Its sociological result was a disenchantment from traditional education, whose categories being embedded in the scriptural and mythological lores had an obsessive degree of orientation towards the past. The categorical structure of the new education was oriented to the present and future. Disciplines like history, geography, political science and economics, etc., in the curricula had a subtle orientation to focus the attention of students on social and physical realities and on the worldview of contemporaneity and anthropocentrism. This itself marked a major break from the traditional outlook and system of values.[11]

In cultural modernization through education often more positive value is associated with learning of physical and biological sciences, medicine and engineering rather than the humanities and social sciences. The reason for this association is not only that science education has more modernizing effects than arts, but because this education creates manpower which is indispensable for economic and industrial growth. Nevertheless, if the creation of a substantial profession in science and engineering contributes to modernization of society, education in the humanities and social sciences contributes to the modernization of man. One must not be considered less significant than the other.[12]

Progress has also been made in other spheres of educational planning and modernization of its organization. Percentage of girls going to schools and colleges has increased. In many states schooling of children has been made free and compulsory. New vocational and polytechnical institutions have been started for better utilization of educated manpower for the economic and social growth of the country.[13]

Yogendra Singh has categorically remarked that "the expansion of education has not led to a sociologically meaningful degree of social mobility and change in stratification system. Higher education is still primarily confined to the upper classes, is a scarce good and reflects the advantages of wealth and social origin."[14]

In spite of these limitations, education has been one of the most influential instruments of modernization in India. It has led to the mobilization of people's aspirations for nationalism, liberalism and freedom. It alone has been responsible for the growth of an enlightened intelligentsia which carried forward not only a movement for independence but also a relentless struggle for social and cultural reforms. It has created a sub-culture of students in India which though not fully modern, contains elements of transition from tradition to modernity. The persistent strains that we find in the internal system of this sub-culture partly reflect the stresses of transition from one constellation of values to another and partly result from the structural maladjustment of this culture with that of the larger society. Yet, its modernizing significance is self-evident. Finally, the educational system has contributed to modernization by growth of new forms of rationally organized structures in the shape of schools, colleges and universities, which serve as cultural networks for the diffusion of knowledge and cultural categories which are modern in ethos. However, some elements of conflict between tradition and modernity can persistently be discerned in the functioning and administration of the educational system in India at all levels. Whereas modernization has in some forms been welcomed there has also been a conscious effort to preserve the traditional values.[15]

Yogendra Singh has pointed out that "this has a very logical explanation. Modernization in all traditional cultures goes along with the process of a new identity consciousness. Since the former is an outer-directed process, the latter must necessarily be inner-directed. Hence, identity consciousness finds its basic symbolic structure in the past tradition. Nationalism, as a modernizing process in such societies emerges as a queer blend of modern psychology of outer-directedness and the commitment to tradition as revealed by inner-directed search for national symbols. In the field of education a good example is the following statement in the report of the Education Commission, 1964-66, appointed by the Government of India:

> 'The most powerful tool in the process of modernization is education based on science and technology. The one great lesson of the present age of science is that with determination and willingness to put in hard work prosperity is within the reach of any nation which has a stable and progressive government. There is no doubt in the years to come India's trade and commerce will grow; there will be more food for all; more education, better health and a reasonable standard of living will be available. But India's contribution can, and should be far more than these material gains. She should learn to harness science but she must also learn not to be dominated by science'."[16]

In our mind, the process of globalization is significant while discussing the modernizing process. The relations between local and global culture, institutionalized changes, changes in social relations, question of identity, and transformation of economy are clearly visible in India. At this point of our discussion on modernization and education we would therefore, like to present the views of Yogendra Singh on the issue of globalization and its impact on Indian society.

Globalization: Its Challenges

Yogendra Singh has expounded that "globalization is a composite process. It results from the convergence of a series of developments in society which are qualitatively new. These include: contemporary revolution in science and technology of communication, high velocity movements of finance, capital and market, increased social mobility, migration of personnel and the emergence of a global diaspora. Its associated contributory processes are: intensification of cultural interaction among diverse groups through media exposure, increased incidence of leisure-time activities, growth in tourism, infrastructures of entertainment and marketing of cultural products, personnel and styles. These developments have an evolutionary character, as they are generally irreversible despite societies going through the cycles of growth and depression in economy, polity and social system. This attribute of globalization has social structural and political consequences which are often overlooked as most treatment of this process has focused upon a segmental rather than a holistic analysis of its nature and consequences".[17]

Yogendra Singh has further explained ideology of globalization in this way: "In my view, globalization is a unique process. It is a product of such developments in the field of science and technology which are entirely new to human history. And, these offer new opportunities to humankind as also pose many challenges. It is a fact, however, that several of its features taken individually did indeed exist in the past, such as international trade by sea and land routes, capitalism and imperialism, market and capital mobility and transfer of workforce from one country to another. But, devoid as these processes in the past were of the advantages of the modern technologies, their total impact upon society and its direction of change was qualitatively different. Therefore, the nature of challenges was also different. Hence, to understand its fuller implications, a new ideological paradigm is necessary. It must be of an interdisciplinary nature, because globalization is a multidimensional and multidirectional process. Its implications have to be understood and analyzed from a holistic perspective. The particularistic perspective, either on the basis of political economy as we find in Marxist-Leninist critique or that of culture, symbols or images as we find in the discourse on post-modernism, remain inadequate. While highlighting some of the aspects of globalization, each one of them leaves a much larger segment of globalization, its nature and consequences etc., unaccounted for. Sociology, to my mind, could be one such discipline which has a broad enough integrative theoretical perspective to offer a paradigm for the analysis of globalization. It focuses upon the study of the 'specific' or local in the perspective of the 'total' and the historical. Its methodology and epistemology offer both variety and flexibility of an approach to deal with social realities that may be 'normal' or 'enigmatic' or paradoxical. Globalization is a good candidate to merit its attention."[18]

Yogendra Singh has explained that "any revolutionary transformation in society brings in its wake both challenges and opportunities. This is true also for globalization. Not that these challenges are confined only to a developing society like India. The developed world is also not immune from them, as it too faces the challenges of globalization; only its character is different. In the developing societies, the tensions and anxieties on account of globalization are primarily economic which spill over to the anxieties about culture and identity. In the developed world, culture seems to top over all other anxieties on account of globalization. In Europe, we witness this in the crescendo of debate on multiculturalism and in the revival of the ideology of the 'right and the radical-cultural exclusiveness'. In India, however, the cultural and ethnic aspects of the challenges of globalization do exist, but these are in most cases derivatives of the anticipated unpredictable consequences to the economy, polity and social structure.

In terms of social structure, India remains essentially a rural-agrarian society. Only about 30 percent of our population is urban and the pace of urbanization remains slow. The addition to our urban population comes mainly from the rural poor, who migrate in search of employment. They remain marginalized in the urban economy and hold the lowest position in the urban social structure. Thus, a major challenge that globalization is likely to pose to our social structure is related to the nature of inequalities in the society. We witness these inequalities at several levels, such as between the village and town, between the middle classes and the working classes, between males and females, between marginalized ethnicities and the dominant castes or communities and between the mobile metropolitan diaspora and the illiterate masses in the villages, urban slums and at the periphery of the tribal lands. How is globalization going to affect these sections of our society? Its pace at present is no doubt measured and slow due to choice of policies and also because of the limitations that our social structure itself imposes upon the pace of globalization, but the challenges are likely to grow and pose serious problems in the future.

The impact of globalization on the structural changes in the society comes generally through the changes in the economic policies. India, since independence, has been following a policy of import-substitution and inward-looking market economy. This policy handicapped the economy in global competitiveness, in the manufacturing sector and in exportable commodity production. But its focus upon higher education in science and technology and agricultural infrastructures did compensate the loss. It is evident in 'green revolution' in agriculture, in our growing strength in the sectors of information technology, the professions, the rising middle classes and in the space research which has added edge to our growth in telephony, television and mass communication. Also, the investment in the capital-intensive sectors, such as steel, petrochemicals, power, etc., have generated an economic and technological potential strong enough to cope up with the exposure to the contemporary challenges of globalization. The existing economic, social and cultural resilience of our society is to a large measure influenced by the rising middle class. It is estimated that by 2020, half of the Indian population would comprise the middle classes even at the contemporary rate of the economic growth! Despite this, the challenges of globalization felt by India in the early 1990's made it inevitable to change these policies. Of course, the difference (see, Herzog, 1999; Malhautra, 2001; Panchamukhi in Chadha, 2001) of opinion on matters related to economic liberalization continues to persist."[19]

Yogendra Singh further writes: "To take these factors into account and yet to encounter the challenges of globalization, an integrated policy is required. Increased export earnings and foreign trade on the one hand, and the need for massive foreign capital investment on the other depend upon how fast we move in this direction both at the federal and the state levels. In foreign trade and export earnings, we have a temporary advantage of low wages and human resources, but economies of scale and technological modernization of the production process are required. Reforms are required in management, governance, labour legislation and fiscal and monetary policies. Capital investment on a massive scale is needed to develop the infrastructures in the sectors of power, roadways, railways, airports and ports, etc. India has lagged behind in foreign capital investment, apart from other reasons also because of our weak infrastructure. Its inadequacy hampers the growth of our trade and modernization of agriculture. No doubt, globalization does create a "mismatch between growth of trade, growth of output and growth of employment" (Panchamukhi in Chadha, 2001: 11), but its negative consequences can certainly be avoided if our infrastructure is modern and our policies with regard to various sectors of economy are adequately synchronized. We may need to reinforce our legal expertise, laws about the intellectual property rights, banking and insurance policies and measures to protect our economy from unfair trade policies from abroad.

Modernization of agriculture is an urgent requirement as 70 percent of our population depends upon it. About 90 percent of employment in our country is offered by the unorganized sector, of which agriculture is a primary component. Studies reveal that during 1990-98 nearly 7 million Indian workers, of which about 4 million in the rural and 3 million in the urban sectors, lost their jobs. Also, the quality of workforce in the rural areas is poor; during 1993-94 NSS round, 44 percent of rural males and 80 percent of rural females were found to be illiterate (see, Chadha, 2001). Hence, the urgent need for the improvement of the rural human resource base of our country. This would reduce the crisis of inequalities in the social and political structure and also strengthen the pace of our economic modernization. The farming sector in our economy has chronically suffered from underdevelopment due to lack of investment and adverse terms of trade and tariff policies. Despite this, globalization has so far not caused any massive dislocation, may be only because of its slow pace in our country or because of our policies. But, eventually, agriculture would have to become commercial and oriented to value added production. This is slowly taking place as some studies reveal (see, Panini, 1999), but its scale is still minuscule due to lack of investment and poverty of infrastructure and human resources.

These challenges of economic globalization have indeed created a social structural crisis of change in our society. The social inequalities have increased in relative terms. But to call it structural dualism may be an oversimplification. The studies on the consumption data indicate that the rural areas constitute about 80-90 percent of the market for the factory-made consumer goods. There exists a strategic linkage between the rural economy and the industrial sector producing consumer goods. A middle class has emerged in the villages and it continues to grow in size.

In bringing about these changes the expansion of the mass media has played an important role. The incidence of telephony, access to radio and television and in some areas even the uses of the internet are linking the rural social structure and economy with the outside world as never before. It reinforces inter-regional and inter-state linkages, alters the character of the social mobility of skilled and unskilled labour and in some measures it also creates inter-regional or inter-state inequalities. These changes have the potential in the long run to influence the nature of social inequalities in our society and also the pattern of political and cultural interactions among groups and regions within and across the states."[20]

Yogendra Singh further writes: "India has been exposed to cultural contacts with other civilization since millennia. It has been continually making adaptive changes in its cultural styles, traits and forms as it encountered other cultures. It has a history of accommodating identities. The cultural impact of globalization on the identity of this civilization or its impact upon the identities of local cultures, therefore, is bound to be mediated by this resilience. There are several reasons for this observation. In the first instance, the initial historical conditions of the Indian social structure have been unique. It is characterized by immense plurality of communities, languages, cultural diacritical symbols and ethnic styles. A variety of cultural traits and cultural styles have, over centuries, given identity to communities but not in total isolation. Cultural interaction among regions and communities has persisted in a mode of co-sharing and mutual accommodation. This commonality has existed beyond the religious and ethnic divides. A recent study by the Anthropological Survey of India illustrates this fact. It observes that the sharing of cultural traits among communities in India, in all about 4,635 in number, shows 'high correlation of traits among states within macro-regions such as those in the south, north-western India and so on. There is very high correlation of traits between the Scheduled Castes and the Scheduled Tribes, between Scheduled Tribes and Hindus, between Hindus and Sikhs, between Hindus and Muslims (which is very high indeed) and between Hindus and Jains. The high correlation between Hindus and Buddhists may also be explained in the same way. This fact that these communities interact across space or states is important'. Thus, we notice that despite the plurality of identities, a macro-linkage of cultural bonds has existed in India throughout history. It continues to subsist even today, and constitutes the cultural unity of India despite plurality of local identities"[21] (Singh, 1992: 99).

Yogendra Singh has explained that "the cultural impact of globalization gets enmeshed within this process of internal dynamics and resilience of the local cultures. The perception that globalization threatens local culture is being increasingly invalidated. It is observed that in the process of globalization, local cultures are reinforced and also globalized. Ronald Robertson has called this process *glocalization*. It indicates how local cultures get increasingly enmeshed with the global culture through selective adaptation of symbolic forms and styles in their products through micro-marketing. Based on the Japanese experience, this process affirms how local cultures begin to occupy a global space by constructing differentiation of consumers. Its examples are witnesses in the field of tourism and the popularity of ethnic supermarkets (see, Robertson, 1994). In India, we witness how our local cultural traditions are also making adaptive responses in the forms and styles of cultural products in tune with the inter-regional and global requirements. For instance, regional languages are being creolized across regions or even in global terms. The incidence of bilingualism has increased in our country from about 13.4 percent in 1971 to 64.2 percent in 1991. The culinary styles, the pattern of dress, local ethnic cultural objects, rituals, religious icons and local customs, etc., are now increasingly becoming pan-Indian and even global due to the increasing size of the Indian diaspora. The process of micro-marketing is penetrating deep into this sphere. The momentum for this is, of course, provided by the emergent forces of economic development. It has triggered a new wave of internal and external migration, and establishes a linkage between culture and market. It also extends the space for cultural interaction as never before. No doubt, it generates a threat perception about cultural identity, but correspondingly it also reinforces the identity consciousness. This ambivalence notwithstanding, the Indian response towards the 'other' cultures has throughout remained selective and adaptive. Globalization is, therefore, leading increasingly towards hybridization or fusion of cultural styles and forms rather than their total displacement. This only shows the strength of cultural resilience of the Indian society."[22]

Yogendra Singh writes: "If we observe the pattern of social mobility and incidence of poverty since independence in our country, we find that measures of social welfare, education and economic development have contributed to the reduction of poverty, but the relative social inequalities have increased. In absolute terms, the standard of consumption has qualitatively improved in villages and towns; the reservation policy together with focus upon education has created a 'limited' middle class among the weaker sections, minorities and ethnic groups; the quality and extent of participation in politics and power sharing by the backward classes, tribes and scheduled castes, etc. has radically changed. A substantial degree of empowerment of these groups has taken place in the political realm, but in the economic and educational fields the gap between them and the dominant classes of castes persists. In my view, globalization does pose challenges on several fronts, foremost of which may be economic. For reasons of history, pluralistic social structure and culture and the democratic path of development that we have adopted, we enjoy tremendous resilience to meet with the challenges of globalization. Notwithstanding this, a cautious fine-tuning and synergy in our economic policies is required. To my mind, the most strategic aspects of such a policy relate to the development of our human resource base, agriculture and infrastructure. Economic development in a balanced manner holds the key to our ability to meet with the challenges of globalization and accommodate the upsurge of identities."[23]

Educational Status of Women

Education is considered both, an end in itself, and as a means to attain certain ends. It develops the personality and wisdom of people, makes them capable of performing certain economic, political and cultural functions and consequently their socio-economic status gets enhanced. Education has been accepted as such an equipment which can be used to forward the process of change and development in society, in the direction of desired goals. It brings mobility in society and helps in bringing equal status among people coming from different social levels. The education system is the only institution which can uproot the deep inequality between men and women; which is settled in the minds of people through the process of socialization.[24]

Under formal education there is a strict bond of specific written rules regarding admission in the educational institutions, teaching and examination, which are to be followed essentially. In order to run a new administrative and economic system, started during the British regime and to fulfil the need of a large number of clerks, schools were opened in different cities, and along with other subjects the students were taught English language. Since Indian women did not have to earn their livelihood, there was no requirement of education for them, though it was being considered. In the beginning, the British government also did not pay any attention towards it because it did not want to interfere with the Indian religious and social system. But the social reformers raised a voice and prior to the government, Christian missionaries and some learned people made efforts in this direction.[25] As Neera Desai has stated, first of all in 1824, in Madras, a girls' school was opened by missionaries in which very few girls came for study. After this, in Bombay in 1949, students' Literary and Scientific Society opened a few morning schools only for two hours, 7-9 a.m. in different areas of the city. The first well established girls' school was opened in Ahmedabad in 1949 by the Gujarat

Vernacular Society, but in that also a very small number of girls took admission. In the field of higher education, in 1857, universities were opened in Calcutta, Madras and Bombay but their doors were closed for girls, which got opened in 1877, and in 1882 two girls could take the graduate degree from Calcutta University. Although the British government had been willing for a long time to make a scheme for educating girls, different aspects of women's education could be considered only in 1882 by the 'Hunter Commission' appointed for this purpose. In 1888, the Commission gave the report that 98 percent girls of school going age were out of school and out of 99.7 million girls 99.5 million girls could not read and write. Due to the custom of veiling, child marriage and household work, many hurdles were coming in the education of girls. It was decided that which ever local institutions wanted to do this work, should be permitted to do so. At this time, municipalities opened many girls' schools.

By 1882, 2,600 primary schools, 81 secondary schools, 15 training schools and one college had been opened. In 1887-88, in Grand Medical College of Bombay, along with medical studies, classes for nurses were also started. At this time in Ahmedabad and Pune, Teacher's Training Colleges were established. Raja Ram Mohan Roy, Ishwar Chandra Vidyasagar, Anne Besant, Saiyed Ahmad Khan, etc. laid emphasis on women's education. At this time specially, conditions in India were changing very fast. The Indian National Congress and Indian National Social Conference, both greatly emphasized the need of women's education. In Bombay and Pune, South Education Society, Pandita Rama Bai, Rama Bai Ranade, D.R. Karve, etc., voluntary organizations and social reformers made efforts and created awareness in this direction. During those days, educational institutions for teaching fine arts to the girls were opening because at that time, women's education through the national language was being emphasized for better performance of their household role.[26]

In 1991-92, more than 3 lakh girls took admission in primary schools but out of them only 2 percent studied up to the secondary level. During 1901-1902, there were 76 girls in medical colleges and 166 girls in medical schools.[27]

In 1902, the Indian University Commission was established. In 1904, Lord Curzon pointed out the lack among education of women and stressed its need. During this time, some progress was made but at a slow speed. During 1907-12, Indian universities gave admission to the outside students also for appearing in the examination. In 1916, under the leadership of Dr. D.K. Karve, in Bombay, SNDT Indian Women's University was established and special subjects were offered for girls, on which different types of restrictions were observed. Dr. Karve had already done this type of experiment in Pune. The University ran a college of 30 girls. Medical education and midwife and nurse training were also arranged. In Delhi also, Lady Hardings Medical College was opened to provide nurse training along with medical education. In this college a university degree in the field of medicine and full training of nursing was provided. In this way, due to awareness of the public during the First World War, the field of education got developed. At this time, owing to the extension of education and health services, in the field of women's education, teaching and medicine, two professions got introduced. In 1921, a decision was taken about giving the education department to the Indian control. In 1921-22, there were 19 colleges, 675 secondary schools and 21,956 primary schools for girls. Owing to the increase in the age of marriage, education got encouraged. The increased demand for educated girls by the educated boys for marriage provided more opportunities for the growth of education. In 1922, there were 197 women in medical college, 334 in medical schools, 67 in teacher's training college and 3,903 in teachers' training schools. Due to the serious efforts of Gandhiji at this time despite the problems of political conflict and economic scarcity education got developed. Due to active participation of women in the

National Freedom Movement, enthusiasm for women's education increased further.[28]

Raghunath Reddy has written that after independence in 1948-49, the University Education Commission was established under the chairmanship of Dr. Radha Krishnan and forwarded many suggestions regarding women's education. In the constitution the promise to provide equal opportunities of education to men and women without any discrimination was already there.[29]

In the directive principles of state policy also, the direction to provide higher education was there. In the field of higher education at this time, urban middle and upper class girls came in a large number because educated boys were demanding girls educated at least up to the graduate level, for marriage. In 1958, under the chairmanship of Mrs. Durga Bai Deshmukh, a national committee was formed for women's education. In 1962, the Hansa Mehta Committee was formed to consider professional education for women and it suggested that they could be taught any subject. In 1964, the Kothari Commission also encouraged the professional syllabus and gave important suggestions. In 1965, under the chairmanship of Sri Bhakta Vatsalam, a committee was appointed to examine the problems of women's education. In 1970, UNESCO celebrated the International Education Year and encouraged women's education. In 1974, the National Committee on the Status of Women also studied the educational Status of Women and reported that the urban middle class was more against co-education than the rural middle class. It suggested providing equal opportunities to girls and boys both, for the study of all types of courses. The United Nations Organization (UNO) celebrated the year 1975, as the 'women's year' and later on declared the period up to 1985 as the women's decade during which like in other countries of the world, in India also, programmes were chalked out to provide new perspectives to women's education.[30]

In the National Education Policy of 1986, provision has been made for free education of the girls up to 14 years of age.

In the new education policy also, women's education has been emphasized. In 1990, the National Women's Commission was established incorporating schemes and programmes regarding women's education. In spite of all these efforts, the girls are still lagging behind boys in the field of education. In 1991, literacy among men was 63.86 percent whereas it was 39.4 percent among women. The difference between the literacy levels of the two categories is about 25 percent. The women's literacy rate shows that even now more than 60 percent women are illiterate. The biggest problem in women's education is dropping out, after taking admission once. Mishra writes that although adequate progress has taken place in the field of women's education and from the beginning of 20th century, their number is increasing, they are still taking less advantage of educational facilities in comparison to boys. International welfare institutions are also providing great help to the Indian government in the field of education, through financial assistance and guidance both. Recently, during the decade 1980-90, the University Grants Commission (UGC) has opened women's study centres in many universities in which three dimensional programmes of teaching, research and fieldwork on women's issues, have to be conducted. For conferences, seminars, workshops, etc., at regional, state, national and international level also, arrangement has been made to provide financial assistance.[31]

Higher education is imparted in the country in 135 universities and various affiliated colleges of arts, science, commerce and professional education. Apart from this, 20 research institutes and other institutions are also working. The UGC, established in 1953, does essential work for the growth and coordination of higher education by determining the standard regarding teaching, examination and research in universities inquiring into and examining their economic needs and giving them sufficient grants, establishing new universities and advising the government on other issues related to higher education. At the state level also, State University Grants

Commissions have been established, which are responsible for proper development of educational institutions and educational standard at state level. Financial assistance is given to colleges run by the voluntary organizations also.[32]

In order to provide opportunities of higher education to the people and to make education the democratic resource available for the people, open universities have been established and programmes of distant learning or correspondence courses at all levels have been introduced.[33]

Saraswati Mishra writes that formal and informal education are being used as a means of bringing basic changes in the standard of women. The national education system is performing a positive interfering role for making women capable. New values are being developed through new syllabi and textbooks with the help of educational institutions, which is necessary to finish the inequalities and deformities continuing from past. In various syllabi studies regarding the status of women are being encouraged. For removing women's illiteracy, those obstacles due to which women cannot complete their education even of the primary level are being cleared off. For this purpose special assistance services are being arranged. At different levels participation of women in technical and professional education for obtaining a livelihood is being emphasized. Different programmes are being implemented among women and the policy against discrimination is being executed with great enthusiasm.[34]

The women studying in universities are only 3 percent of the total female population. But, the size of this section of educated women is so large that it can be considered important. Even though at different levels of higher education the admission of girls has increased, still in all the subjects. A noticeable difference between the number of girls and the number of boys can be observed. Regarding this, whatever little difference has come during last few years is that in technical education, industrial institutes and commerce faculty more girls have taken admission. They very rarely study at engineering and polytechnic colleges. Now the number of girls working as managers, accountants and clerks is increasing therefore the number of girls studying commerce is also gradually increasing. In 1971, the number of girl commerce graduates was 72.84, which became 1,02,564 in 1982-83. Due to modernization of our economic system, opportunities of employment are available for technical trained persons. Therefore, in spite of many social and cultural barriers, girls are studying technical and industrial training courses. On the other hand, it is sad that their number in the medical faculty is decreasing.[35]

Problems Regarding Women's Education

Saraswati Mishra has rightly explained the problems regarding women's education, particularly in India. Mishra writes that, in spite of unprecedented progress in the field of women's education after independence, the situation is that even now lots of efforts are to be made in this direction. Out of the main problems connected with this situation, the first one is widespread illiteracy even now. Out of every three girls only two girls attends classes V to VIII at school. Out of five girls only one girl attend classes I to V at school and at the higher secondary level, out of every eight girls only one girl goes to school. Looking after the younger brother or sister at home, household work, bringing water and firewood from outside, working in other houses to earn a livelihood, etc., are done mostly by girls of lower class families in the villages and cities, therefore, they cannot be sent for studies.

The second problem is that the dropout rate, i.e., leaving the school after enrolment during studies, is also very high among girls. They are admitted to schools with great enthusiasm, but later on when the family members face difficulties with tasks inside the home, they are taken out of schools and their studies get terminated.

After getting the girls educated just up to the primary level, their parents are satisfied with the achievement and their studies are stopped. By the time a girl finishes her 8th class studies, she becomes 14 years old and due to her insecurity in her youth and the preparations for her marriage, her education in higher secondary classes is obstructed. At this level, their education is not considered important, therefore at this level their enrolment remains only 12 percent of their total number. In urban areas, high school education for is limited only up to the higher and middle classes even now.

In rural areas, mainly financially well-off families of the middle class take advantage of studies in higher classes. In rural areas in higher classes girls form not even one-fifth, that is, 20 percent of the total number of students. Thus, the all-India average of dropouts at different levels of education has remained very high among girls in comparison to that among boys. At the university level, the ratio of girls is higher at postgraduate level rather than at the undergraduate level. The reason for this fact may be that boys take to employment after graduation while the girls keep on studying till their marriage. Since higher education in India is limited to a very small section of people even now, if the total situation is considered, the impact of this tendency on the educational development of women cannot be considered quite sufficient.

Thus, out of the students passing the school examination, per 1,000 boys, the growth rate of the number of girls is comparatively slow. At the level of the first university degree the growth rate of this number is comparatively fast. Higher education of women in comparison to other sections is generally limited up to the urban higher and middle classes.

In the field of women's education, one more problem is their concentration in the study of certain particular subjects. Due to lack of career orientation and consequently, the absence of aptitude, few girls study mathematics and science less even at school level. In the field of professional education, before independence, for the girls only medical, nursing, education and law courses were available because it was believed that they would be able to perform well in these professions. After independence, keeping in mind the principle of equality, opportunities were made available to them for the study of all the subjects. But, in spite of the facilities for studying engineering, industrial, agricultural, commerce courses, etc., their interest in the study of these subjects and its usage in professions have not increased even now. Therefore, more girls take admission in teaching, medical and fine arts courses than in other fields.

The National Committee on Women's Education had suggested establishing separate educational institutions for girls in order to end the prejudice regarding girls' education, because most parents do not want to educate them with boys in the same institution. Therefore, during the period after 1960-61 the number of girls' institutions increased very fast and even in 1967-68, out of the total number of institutions, 29 percent were established for girls only, compared to 10 percent in 1947-48. It has also been always accepted that for development of women's education, increasing the number of female teachers is a compulsory condition.[36]

The main obstacles can be classified under two heads, 'social' and 'economic'. The two pernicious practices of child marriage and 'purdah' are responsible for many evils in the country. Information regarding girls is much more difficult to obtain than information regarding boys. There is, in fact, a hereditary custom to give no information regarding women of the household. There are two other very important problems that have to be discussed in connection with women's education, viz., co-education and curriculum. In urban areas, the belief in women's education has been realized. It is, however, in the vast rural areas of this country that the problems of education present tremendous difficulties.

There is also a third factor, and that is the lower status of women in the family. In fact, the backwardness of Indian women's education is largely due to our social and economic conditions as well as the lack of a clear perception of the aims and ideals of education.

Marginalization of women from the mainstream socio-economic, political and cultural scenario is mainly due to gender-biases in the educational institutions, options for education, training available to girl students and employment opportunities available to the educated and qualified women. If less educated and untrained women occupy the decision-making bodies, they have to depend mostly on men (with all their anti-women prejudices) for their day-to-day functioning. If highly qualified women have no mandatory power, their talent remains unutilized or under-utilized and in due course of time, they become cretins. If we want to avoid both these situations, we will have to examine the monolithic structures of the formal educational institutions with their class, caste, communal and sexist biases and provide concrete alternatives in terms of:

(a) an increased outreach of the educational (both of formal and non-formal variety) institutions,
(b) reforms in the existing curricula with commitment to social justice, gender justice, communal harmony and peaceful governance, and
(c) more allocation of resources in terms of land, money and human resources.[37]

The reason for the recent enthusiasm about women's education in the official discourse is due to the fact that several area studies have shown that educated women are able to avoid child marriage, command more autonomy in their reproductive rights and produce less number of children.[38]

Women's Education: Change in Attitudes

Saraswati Mishra observes that, although in rural areas even now traditional attitudes and behaviour persist towards female education, the attitudes and behaviour of urban higher and middle class people are changing very fast. By considering education very important in solving the problems of life, girls are being given higher education and quite a few of them are allowed to take up employment also. Earlier, it was thought that girls have less capability and aptitude to study subjects like mathematics and science, in comparison to boys, but now their success in various examinations in comparison to boys, has eradicated this concept. In the field of professional education, they are taking admission in subjects like engineering, industry, agriculture, law, etc. besides the medical and education fields whereas earlier they used to go for these mostly. Now, education is not considered an end but the means of earning livelihood. Before independence very few women, and that too only those forced by the conditions of economic hardship, used to go out of the four walls of the house and involve themselves in money earning occupations and activities. Working women used to be considered against the honour of the family and they were also looked down upon. Therefore, girls used to take education in order to get an educated and financially well off husband, and if required, to become financially independent during any emergency in life. But now this attitude is changing and parents have also started selecting the subjects for education as well as the field of profession for their daughters as they do for their sons. Especially in the case of intelligent girls it is a fact that for their education, special facilities are made available inside and outside the home. Earlier, a girl used to pose an obstruction in her marriage; therefore, they had to choose between marriage or a profession and advance in that direction. As a result, most girls active professions had to remain unmarried throughout their life. But now it is not so and by making adjustment in both the fields, adopting a balanced lifestyle is possible these days. Now, a working woman is considered an honour for the family and family members provide assistance and cooperation to her in various ways. Quite a few women take education even after marriage and put it to use.

Due to rising prices and ambition of a higher standard of living, today educated boys of the lower middle class wish to marry educated working girls. In spite of having no economic requirement, women of higher class families are becoming active in some profession due to their desires to become financially independent, have their own identity, achieve high status and realise self-respect, etc. Higher education is considered as a big achievement and symbol of modernization now. By understanding the difficulties of working wives, educated sensible husbands do not expect an excellent performance in household roles from them and provide them assistance to cope with the double roles they perform.

Owing to the higher age for marriage also, girls are able to get education. In cities, free mobility of girls in society is being approved of and various social restrictions on them are being relaxed. In rural areas also, getting girls of higher middle class families, educated up to school level is considered a very important task for parents. Later on, early marriages pose a restriction for education of higher level because most girls are married before the age of twenty years. For the highly educated girl a more highly educated young man is required for marriage, for which a lot of dowry is expected. In this way, parents have to spend a double amount, i.e., on education and on the marriage of their daughter. Due to this reason also girls are not given higher education. In the lower class, urban and rural both, indifferent attitude towards women's education exits even now. In this class, some people think of giving no education at all to girls whereas most of them do not want to give them higher education. In the lower class now, sending the wife outside the house to earn money is being considered against the honour of the husband. Therefore, they are unable to understand the utility of education. They feel that the training in household jobs that they get right since childhood can be used anytime in life to earn a livelihood when required. Due to a lack of desire for a very high standard of life, without education life can be maintained; therefore, in spite of special facilities provided by the government, lower class people do not benefit them, especially in rural areas.

The impact of educational growth can be observed specially in urban areas. Most of the girls of all social classes are taking education in schools. Girls of higher and middle classes are advancing towards the adoption of career oriented lifestyle after taking higher education. Quite a few married and unmarried women of these classes are engaged now in various professions. In every field women are working shoulder to shoulder with men successfully and they have proved that they are not any less capable than men. The most prominent impact of education is seen in society in the form of the establishment of new values of equality between men and women due to which change in behaviour is also observed. In educated families, believing in the values of equality, an educated girl is considered to be an asset and not a liability. An educated wife today is not considered the slave of her husband but a companion and friend. This change has started only among the urban educated higher and middle class people and its speed is quite slow. But as education extends to the rural areas and among lower class people, these impacts will certainly be created. Along with improvement of women's status through education, progress and development of society have also gained speed, due to their social, economic and political participation.[39]

Education that inculcates human and spiritual values is of great significance for the empowerment of women. These are needed not only in educational institutions but in every walk of life and throughout the world where mankind exists. India has produced great women and they have even ruled the country for some time. What is needed is to see that the entire population is involved in creating a sense of awareness about the need to empower women through quality education including value education. Only a couple of examples may not keep the community comfortable. One has to watch and see the progress of the country in all spheres.[40]

Educated women are thus a microscopic minority in our society. Very few women in our society receive college and university education. It is expected that this minority which benefits from the educational institutions, will play an important role in the social, economic and political life of the country.

The Present Study: Objectives

The present study is a systematic investigation into the indices of modernity as found in urban community life in Darbhanga district of Bihar state. This study is confined to a particular section or category of people. The universe under study is the group of educated women residing and working in Darbhanga. It is evident from the fact that this section is exposed to various factors and forces of modernization and at the same time, it is linked with the traditional family and social structure.

In traditional Indian society, women were confined to household affairs and according to traditional and religious sanctions it was obligatory on their part to serve their father in the pre-marital period, the husband after marriage and the sons in the latter part of married life. Outdoor activities were beyond the jurisdiction of Indian women. They were not allowed to participate in politics and economic affairs of society. But in modernized society, in the present age women are participating in outdoor activities like men. The discrimination on sex basis has been done away with. The concept of equality of the two sexes is widely propagated and honoured.

The women under study are those who are not confined to domestic life. They have received education for a number of years. They have also been exposed to the system of education at graduate and postgraduate levels. They have faced interview boards consisting of men on different occasions. They are employed in imparting education to the younger generation. Hence, they have been facing both, boys as well as girls in the class rooms. In the colleges imparting education up to the postgraduate level, they work not only with female teachers but also with male teachers. In other occupations also, they face male members at their work place. Hence, they are exposed to different conditions and circumstances. All these facts are the negation of traditional factors and forces and are helpful in developing a liberal and rational outlook and contributing to the process of modernization. In the background of the factors promoting rationalization of attitudes and modernization of approaches, the study of modernization of this section of woman population is quite significant.

Economic dependence of women on men has been a dominant feature of traditional Indian society. Under this system men were expected to earn and women were required to manage household affairs. This complete financial dependence of women on men was a source of exploitation of women in traditional Indian society. They were treated like a commodity or possession and lived under the authoritarian control of the patriarch. They did not play any role in family decisions and were expected to obey their husbands or family elders. But earning by women has changed the situation altogether. It has led to the development of economic independence or at least economic inter-dependence in family life. It is believed that employment of women in the world outside is an index of emancipation, a factor leading to the rationalization of social structure. Women working as college and university teachers or with some other status are not only employed or earning hands; they occupy a respectable status in society as well. They are not required to look towards their masters for initiative or decision. They are mature and capable enough to understand a complicated problem and to sort it out. Their education and occupation are expected to develop self-confidence in them. They are expected to be rational in their approach. Thus, the nature of the job, the place of the job in society and the self-confidence developing among women are expected to be favourable to the development of a modern outlook. Hence, another objective of the study is to find out the extent to which these women have been modernized in the existing favourable circumstances.

In traditional Indian society, women were confined to domestic affairs and were not treated at par with men. In modern society, sex discrimination has ended and women are also receiving education and working in different capacities. The educated working women covered by this study are employed in different institutions on respectable posts. Thus, employment itself is an index of modernity. But how far this index of modernity has produced its impact on other aspects of socio-cultural life and attitudes and personalities of these women is an important point to be noted in this study.

The caste system has been deeply rooted in traditional Indian society and social life moves around the pivot of caste. This system is characterised by non-recognition of personal qualities, rigid caste hierarchy and caste endogamy. On the other hand, modernity demands the recognition of personal qualities, flexible stratification and freedom for the choice of the life partner. For the study of modernization, it is important to find out whether educated women are still committed to traditional sanctions or have adopted a modern outlook. Hence, another objective is to know the views and attitudes of women about caste endogamy and inter-caste marriage, that is, whether they still stick to the principle of marriage within the caste, or favour the idea of inter-caste marriages against traditional sanctions.

Moreover, the study also aims at discovering whether people are still in favour of the continuance of a rigid caste hierarchy, placing the Brahmin at the top or they are opposed to it. In many parts of Indian society, non-Brahmin castes have become dominant castes and in actual practice the traditional hierarchy has weakened. It is to be seen whether these women favour this mobility in caste or they choose to see the continuance of the traditional system? In addition to this, in traditional society, marriages were negotiated and settled by parents or guardians and the partners concerned accepted their decisions. But in the present age, the moderate or liberal outlook favours the fixation of marriage by parents with the consent of the partners concerned. In extreme cases, the approval of the parents is not at all needed and the partners concerned choose their mates themselves and get married.

Hence, these different forms of choice of mates and marriage indicate different points on the tradition-modernity continuum and the views of the people may reflect where they stand in this continuum. Consequently, the analysis of this aspect has also been in this study.

The rapid growth of population has created an alarming situation in the country. The problem of overpopulation has given birth to a number of problems like unemployment, under-employment, low living standard, existence of a considerable section below poverty line and the poor economic condition of the masses. Rationality demands a check on population meet the present crisis. Hence, the adoption of birth control measures and the practice of family planning have become essential from the modern point of view. But the tradition-oriented people dominated by religious orthodoxy are opposed to it because of the view that religion does not permit it and it is against religious sanctions. The study also aims at finding out the views and attitudes of educated women regarding family planning and other health issues.

Another important objective of the study is to find out the degree of political socialization and the extent of political participation of educated women in the democratic process. Democracy or mass participation and modernization are positively correlated. A higher degree of political socialization and participation in political activities suggests a higher degree of modernization.

Exposure to mass media is directly related to the modernization process. Newspapers, books, journals, magazines, radio programmes, TV channels are playing major roles in this direction. Higher degrees of exposure serve as the indices of modernization. The study also aims at finding out the degree of exposure of the people to these mass media in understanding the extent of their acceptance of modern values.

This study is concerned with Indian women who have been exploited in the past and have remained an underprivileged, backward and deprived section of the traditional society.

But the educated women represent the progressive section of womanhood and show the emancipation of Indian women. The prime hypothesis of this study is to find out how educated women are exposed to the modernization process and to what extent they have been modernized.

Darbhanga District: The Setting

Darbhanga is one of the northern districts of Bihar. It is bound on the north by Madhubani district, on the south by the district of Samastipur, on the east by Saharsa district and the west by the districts of Muzaffarpur and Sitamarhi. According to the Gazetteer, it takes its name from its chief town and local patriotism insists that Darbhanga is derived from Dwar-Banga (Diara-Banga) or Dar-I-Banga, meaning the door of Bengal. This derivation appears, however, to be philologically impossible and also historically incorrect, as the division between Bengal and Bihar has always been much further to the east. It seems more probable that the name is derived from that of the traditional founder of the town, one Darbhangi Khan, a Mohammedan free booter, of whom little or nothing is known. Until 1875, it was a part of Tirhut district. The total area of the district is 2,279 sq. kms. The sub-division as Darbhanga Sadar had been created earlier in 1845. Now, the trimmed Darbhanga district has two sub-divisions, viz., Darbhanga Sadar and Benipur consisting of 12 development blocks in all. The main languages spoken in the district are Maithili, Urdu and Hindi. Darbhanga is a parliamentary constituency along with assembly segments.

The total population of the district according to the 1991 census is 25,10,959 persons, comprising of 13,13,974 males and 11,96,985 females. The rural population of the district is 22,92,568 persons (11,97,059 males and 1,09,509 females). The SC and the ST population of the district as per 1991 census was 3,65,542 persons and 259 persons respectively.

The land of the region of Darbhanga consists of a great alluvial plain with a general slope from north to south, altered by a depression in the centre. This region lies on a low level, in many places indented with chains of shallow marshes marking the lines of drainage by which the local rainfall and the overflow of the hill streams which intersect the district find their way southwards to the Ganges. According to available information, the soil pattern of this region may be divided into three types, viz., Balsundri (a sandy loam), Bangar or Chikna (a clayey soil with an admixture of sand) and Mativari (a clayey soil with little or no sand).

The principal crops of this region are Aghani (winter crops when varieties of paddy are harvested). However, the general crops of this region may fall under three main harvests, viz., the Aghani, the Bhadai and the Rabi. The Aghani is the winter crop which is harvested in the months of Aghan and Push (December-January). The Bhadai is the early autumn crop which is reaped and harvested in the months of Bhado (August-September). The Rabi crops include such cold weather crops as wheat, pulses, etc. In addition to these crops, the people of Mithila region also produce sugarcane, tobacco, jute, etc. There are a few water crops which include 'Makhana' and 'Singhara'. Makhana is a very popular and profitable money crop as it is sold at hundred to one hundred and twenty rupees per kg. The most important commodity which is exported to other places from Darbhanga and Madhubani is Makhana. Most interestingly, fish is a favourite item of food for the people of Darbhanga. Fish and rice is the staple diet of the people. This district is one of the principal fish producing centres in Bihar. The old-time industry which is still continuing in the district, the production of sugar. The sugar industry has not only survived but has also become one of the important industries in the district and consumes the large output of sugarcane in the district. It also draws supplies from beyond the district. There are, however, no mining or heavy industries in this district except the Ashoka Paper Mill.

Darbhanga district has a well-knit communication system. It is served by the North Eastern Railway, has a sound system of roadways and considerable boat traffic in the bigger rivers. The district has a good number of roads, half of which are tarmacked including the state highways. The district has a landing ground. However, there is no regular air service in the district. The district has many temples and centres of tourism. Kusheshwar Asthan and Videshwar Asthan are the most popular sacred places among them.

Darbhanga town attained the status of a city (population one lakh and above) in 1961. It is the seat of the Maharaja of Darbhanga. Laheriasarai which is the seat of the district and divisional administration is a part of Darbhanga town. The Raj area is well developed and consists of a beautifully laid-out complex of palaces, temples, offices, parks, gardens and ponds. There are a number of palaces built by successive Maharajas, important among them being Nargauna palace, Anandbagh palace and Bela palace.

The 'Darbhanga Raj' came into existence through education and knowledge from the Great Akbar and now, a number of main buildings of the Raj are being used by Kameshwar Singh Darbhanga Sanskrit University and Lalit Narayan Mithila University, Darbhanga for higher education and knowledge. The old Raj library has been taken over by the great patrons of art and literature and through their magnificence, has always provided encouragement to scholars of Maithili and Sanskrit.

Lalit Narayan Mithila University, Kameshwar Singh Darbhanga Sanskrit University and a medical college known as DMCH are centres for higher education. The town has many colleges. C.M. College and C.M. Science College and M.R.M. College are the most prestigious institutions in the field of higher education. In the town, there are many other institutions in the field of science, management and information technology. The town has a Doordarshan Kendra and an AIR station.

Methodology

For this study, a systematic method was needed and hence it was necessary to prepare a research design for the purpose. It is evident that different types of study designs are used in different situations for the present study. Here, we use 'multiple methodologies' for studying the impact and process of modernization among the educated women of Darbhanga district.

The study is confined only to Darbhanga district. It is obvious that the universe is very large. So scientifically here we use the sampling method for the study.

The study has involved methods of sociological repertory. It involved fieldwork carried out to collect data on 200 cases of highly educated women belonging to different categories. As regards the materials, the information has been gathered from both documentary and field sources through various techniques such as observation, interview-schedules, etc.

The field observations were made from different perspectives, depending upon the situation. In the organization and analysis of the data collected, several steps were undertaken to maintain accuracy. Screening was first done to delete unwanted materials. Through the editing operation, checks were made in the original framework of the study and data were collected. In classification, the categories in the proper settings were formed for presenting the data. Thus, the analysis or the creative part of research was done stepwise to draw systematic inferences in a sequential form. The results were finally translated into conceptual language.

Highly Educated Women: Social Profile

The empirical situation as regards the prevalence of varying degrees of modernity and the extent to which the process of modernization had spread its roots among the highly educated women in Darbhanga district has been the basis of this study.

As regards the age composition of the sample under study, it was observed that 32.5 percent of the women belonged to the age group of 21-30, 40 percent of the women belonged to the age group of 31-40, 24 percent of the women belonged to the age group of 41-50 and 3.5 percent of the women belonged to the age group of 51 years and above.

The place of birth of 60 percent of the women was in a rural areas whereas 40 percent women belonged to the urban.

As regards caste background, 60 percent of the women belonged to the higher castes, 22.5 percent of the women belonged to the middle castes and 10 percent belonged to the lower castes. In addition to these caste groups, there is a category of 'other religion'. About 7.5 percent of the women belonged to this category. This category includes women belonging to Muslim, Christian and Sikh religions. The remaining women belonged to the Hindu religion.

As regards the educational qualifications of women, it is obvious that all the women are highly educated. The majority of the women (58%), were holding the Bachelor's degree, 31 percent of the women had the Master's degree and 11 percent women had the Doctoral degree. Among the higher castes, 35 percent of the women are holding the Bachelor's degree, 17.5 percent of the women had the Master's degree and 7.5 percent of women had the Doctoral degree. Among the middle castes, 13 percent of the women had the Bachelor's degree, 8.5 percent of the women had the Master's degree and 2.5 percent of the women had the Doctoral degree. Among the lower castes, 6 percent of the women were holding Bachelor's degree, 2.5 percent of women had the Master's degree and not even a single woman had the Doctoral degree. Among the category of 'other religion', 4 percent of the women were holding the Bachelor's degree, 2.5 percent of the women were holding the Master's degree and only 1.5 percent of the women were holding the Doctoral degree.

It means that the attitude of society towards women's education was changing. Even women belonging to the middle and lower castes were struggling for better education.

As regards the occupational status, the sample includes working women, women in business, women students and housewives. Around 67.5 percent of the women were in service, 10 percent of the women were in business, 7.5 percent of the women were studying in the colleges and in the university departments. About 15 percent women were not working outside but they were working as housewives within their homes.

As regards the income (per month), 45.1 percent of the women were earning one thousand to ten thousand rupees, 32.2 percent of the women were earning ten thousand one to fifteen thousand rupees, 9.6 percent of the women were earning one thousand one to five thousand, the same percentage of 9.6 percent of the women were earning fifteen thousand one to twenty thousand and only 3.2 percent of the women were earning twenty thousand one rupees and above. The above mentioned data represents the earning from a job or from business. So, the total n=155 (77.5%) women were earning. 22.5 percent women were not earning because they were either studying or were housewives.

As regards the marital status, 12.5 percent of the women were unmarried, 82.5 percent of the women were married the and remaining 5 percent of the women were widows or separated or divorced. It means that the majority of the women were leading married life. As regards the types of marriage, majority of women's (91.4%) marriages were arranged. Only 8.5 percent of women's marriages were love marriages.

As regards composition of the family, 80 percent of the women were living in nuclear families, whereas only 20 percent of the women were living in joint families. It is clear that the traditional joint family is disintegrating. As regards size of the family, 60 percent of the women have a family size up to four members, 35 percent of the women have a family size of five to eight members, whereas only 5 percent of the women were found living in big families with nine members or more.

It is in the backdrop of the above social profile of the women that the study of the extent of modernization and its impact on these highly educated women was conducted in the Darbhanga district of Bihar.

Notes

1. S.S. Mathur, *A Sociological Approach to Indian Education*, Vinod Pustak Mandir, Agra, 1997, p. 73.
2. Ibid.
3. Yogendra Singh, *Modernization of Indian Tradition*, Rawat Publications, 1988 (Reprint), Jaipur, p. 61.
4. Ibid., pp. 61-62.
5. Yogendra Singh, *Culture Change in India: Identity and Globalization*, Rawat Publications, Jaipur and New Delhi, 2000, pp. 21-23.
6. Yogendra Singh, *Indian Sociology: Social Conditioning and Emerging Concerns*, Rawat Publications, Jaipur and New Delhi, 1986, pp. 77-78.
7. Yogendra Singh, 1988 (Reprinted), op. cit., p. VII.
8. Ibid., pp. 101-2.
9. Ibid., p. 102.
10. B.B. Mishra, 1960, Supra, pp. 302-5.
11. Yogendra Singh, op. cit., p. 103.
12. Ibid., p. 103.
13. Ibid., p. 105.
14. Ibid., pp. 105-6.
15. Ibid., p. 106.
16. Ibid., pp. 106-7.
17. Yogendra Singh, *Ideology and Theory in Indian Sociology*, Rawat Publications, Jaipur and New Delhi, 2004, p. 206.
18. Ibid., pp. 210-11.
19. Ibid., pp. 211-13.
20. Ibid., pp. 213-15.
21. Ibid., pp. 216-17.
22. Ibid., pp. 217-18.
23. Ibid., p. 219.
24. Saraswati Mishra, *Status of Indian Women*, Gyan Publishing House, New Delhi, 2002, p. 68.

25. Neera Desai, *Women in Modern India*, Vohra and Company, Bombay, 1977.
26. Saraswati Mishra, op. cit., pp. 70-71.
27. Ibid., p. 71.
28. Ibid., pp. 71-72.
29. Raghunath Reddy, *Changing Status of Educated Working Women*, B.R. Publishing Corporation, Delhi, 1986.
30. Saraswati Mishra, op. cit., pp. 72-73.
31. Ibid., p. 74.
32. Ibid., pp. 75-76.
33. Ibid., p. 77.
34. Ibid., pp. 78-79.
35. Ibid., pp. 82-83.
36. Ibid., pp. 84-87.
37. Vibhuti Patel, *Women's Challenges of the New Millennium*, Gyan Publishing House, New Delhi, 2002, p. 85.
38. Roger Jeffery and Alka M. Basu, *Girls' Schooling, Women's Autonomy and Fertility Change in South Asia*, Sage Publications, New Delhi. 1996,
39. Saraswati Mishra, op. cit., pp. 87-90.
40. Sethumadhava Rao, P.H., *Education for Women's Empowerment in Empowering the Indian Women*, Dr. Promilla Kapur (ed.), Publication Division, Ministry of Information and Broadcasting, Government of India, New Delhi, 2001, pp. 54-55.

References

Chadha, G.R., "India and WTO: Some Suggestions for International Corrections and External Initiatives", in Chadha, G.R. (ed.), *WTO and the Indian Economy*, New Delhi: Deep and Deep Publications, 2001.

Dube, S.C., *Contemporary India and Its Modernization*, Vikas Publishing House, New Delhi, 1973.

Eisenstadt, S.N., "Modernization: Growth and Diversity", *Indian Quarterly*, 20: 17-42, 1964.

Herzog, S., "Globalization and Poverty Alleviation in India", *Liberal Times*, March 1999.

Kothari, R., *Caste in Indian Politics*, Orient Longman, New Delhi, 1970a.

—, *Politics in India*, Orient Longman, New Delhi, 1970b.

Malhautra, M., (ed.), *New Century: Whose Century?* New Delhi: UBSPD, 2001.

Panchamukhi, V.R., "World Trade Organization and India: Challenges and Perspectives", in Chadha, op. cit.

Panini, M.N., "Trends in Cultural Globalization: From Agriculture to Agribusiness in Karnataka", *Economic and Political Weekly*, July 31, 1999.

Robertson, R., "Globalization or Glocalization?", *Journal of International Communication*, Vol. 1, No. I, 1994.

Singer, Milton, *When a Great Tradition Modernizes: An Anthropological Approach to Indian Civilization*, Vikas, Delhi, 1972.

Singh, K.S., *People of India: An Introduction*, Calcutta: Anthropological Survey of India, 1992.

Singh, Vinita and Kali Nath Jha, "Emerging Professionals: Saleswomen in Ranchi", paper presented in the 'XXIX All India Sociological Conference', Udaipur, December 21-23, 2003.

—, "Process of Globalization: A Study of Tribal Women Students in Ranchi", paper presented in the Golden Jubilee Seminar on 'Anthropology and the Challenge of Development in Jharkhand', Department of Anthropology, Ranchi University, Ranchi and Anthropological Survey of India, January 19-21, 2004.

—, "Migration of Tribal Women from Jharkhand: The Price of Development", paper presented in the National Seminar on 'Tribes, State Policies and NGOs', organized by Indian Anthropological Association, New Delhi, March 26-27, 2004.

Singh, Yogendra, *Essays on Modernization in India*, Manohar, New Delhi, 1978.

—, *Culture Change in India: Identity and Globalization*, Rawat Publications, Jaipur and New Delhi, 2000.

Srinivas, M.N., *Social Change in Modern India*, Berkeley: California University Press, 1966.

Tangri, Shanti S., *Intellectuals and Society in Nineteenth Century India*, Comparative Studies in Society and History, Vol. 3, 1960-61.

2

Modernization: Concept and Process

One of the most significant developments after World War II is the emergence of Afro-Asian countries as independent sovereign nations. All these countries are struggling to transform their social, political and economic systems from traditional folkways and agriculture predominance to modern, ever changing technologies and industrial production. The success of these attempts depends on a variety of factors such as the growth of an institutional framework that is flexible and powerful enough to meet the public's demands, a series of inter-connected social and psychological changes that after traditional behaviour and perspectives, and economic growth. Social scientists have conducted studies to find out possible correlations between these factors and their impact on the process of social change and modernization. These studies have revealed that despite divergent political and social patterns, all the regimes in the newly emerged nations face certain common problems: nationalism, the formation of viable political communities, political participation, lack of education and mass media channels, and above all a determined national will to overcome some of these problems.[1]

Modernization may be defined as "the revolutionary change leading to transformation of a traditional or pre-modern society into the types of technology and associated social organization that characterised the advanced, economically prosperous and relatively politically stable nations of the western world".[2] This remark suggests that the change in the structure and the organization of a society from a traditional to a scientifically based society is called modernization. When a society characterised by superstitions, ignorance and orthodox conservatism is transformed into a society which is technologically oriented and scientifically assumed, the process is called modernization. The model of modernization is not one and uniform throughout human society. Hence, modernization is not concerned with only one particular form of social life; the acceptance of western culture is not the index of modernity or the only indicator of modernization. The models of modernization are different in countries like USA, USSR, Germany and UK. Moreover, Japan is an Asian country which is highly modernized in this century where modernization is not westernization or acceptance of the culture of the west.[3] There is a tendency among some people to accept whatever is prevalent in the west as an indicator of modernization. They try to adopt the western ways of life, language, modes of dress and fashions. But modernization is not westernization. It is not all that which is there in the west. The reasons for this viewpoint are many. First, we cannot say that the whole of the west has the same or a similar model to be followed. A model coming from USSR, or UK or Germany may differ in many vital points. Belief in freedom of individual in UK materially differs from the faith of a classless society in USSR. Secondly, not everything in western living and thinking is good. Two destructive wars have been fought in this century due to the incompatibility of different points of view even though all the nations which fought were western, using the scientific innovations for making themselves rich. Many values of the west may not suit a different culture of a country. Thirdly, Japan is a non-western nation and it offers much to be accepted. It has a modernized society. Thus, modernization is not the exclusive domain of the western nations. Fourthly, no nation should lose its identity; accepting everything of the west will destroy the cultural heritage of the society which adopts them. This is what we mean by modernization.[4] The process of modernization is not independent of the culture and social values of the society in which modernization takes place. It is always in relation to the cultural heritage and social values as well as the ideology prevalent in the society. It was the difference in the cultural heritage and social values of USA and USSR that was responsible for the development of two different models of modernization. In the present age, these two different models of modernization are based upon two broader ideologies known as Marxism and capitalism. Referring to these two different models of modernization, Yogendra Singh has remarked that Marxism and capitalism are two dominant ideologies of our time which outline two ends of a continuum on which a multitude of variations on ideological themes of modernization has been formulated. If we define ideology as the generalised normative construct for the total system of societies (with varying degrees of consensus about it based on differences of wealth, privilege and power) then the controversy about modernization being a structural or cultural notion or about the relative advantages of approaching the study of modernization from a structural, existential or purely normative or cultural frame of reference seems to be contrived rather than real. The value of this distinction may be more on the emphasis on the nature of heuristic variables than on the substantive realities or their fundamental processes in society. The distinction between the Marxist and the capitalist models of modernization cannot be maintained on the basis of the formulation that the former uses variables for analysis that are mostly structural and the later those that are cultural or normative. This fallacy can easily be exposed if one examines the writings of several western sociologists whose analysis of modernization is anchored on capitalist ideological foundations but who use primary structural variables for understanding this process in industrial or post-industrial societies.[5]

The models of modernization under the Marxist and the capitalist ideologies can be distinguished from each other in terms of the ideological framework. The differences in the two models are closely related to two sets of ideologies. But it does not mean that the Marxist model is exclusively based on structural variables and capitalistic model is based only on cultural or normative variables. Both types of variables may be found in the two models. The differences lie in the fact that there is a greater degree of emphasis on structural process in Marxist ideology and there is a greater degree of stress on cultural process in the capitalist model. This fact has been explained by Yogendra Singh: "The primary ideology in the understanding of modernization as a structural or cultural process is derived from the fact that it is intrinsic to the very notion of structure and culture in social science. This is not to say that Marxist model of modernization is based on the primacy of variables of social structure to the exclusion of the variables of culture, and the reverse is true in the capitalist model of modernization. Basic to the two models, however, is the distinctive formulation of social structure or culture as concept for understanding modernization. This distinction is derived basically from the ideological systems that the two models represent".[6]

Due to development in technology, the mode of production changed and improved. Marx viewed a dialectical process between technology and the system of production. He analysed the dialectical process through the stages of affirmation, negation and reconciliation. This process is repeated time and again as history proceeds. In this way, Karl Marx viewed history as a continuous process of conflict between opposites. Thus, he viewed historical continuity through a dialectical process. Hence, the analysis of the concept of modernization is also linked with historical dialectics and historical continuity. According to Marxist ideology, modernization is a process governed by historical dialecticism. Yogendra Singh has remarked that "modernization as a process of change in societies is governed equally by this historical dialectics in which the process of transformulation of societies and culture is linked both to continuation of traditional activities under changed circumstances, adaptive process of change, and modification of the old circumstances with new activities that is innovative change in the words of Marx and Engels. The dialectics of social life is governed by the essentially historical character of both social structure and culture, the former having its roots in existential needs of mankind and their institutional formation and reformation and the latter being the signification or symbolization of the 'essences' of these existentially related social formation in society, in different moments of time. Intrinsic to the historical character of culture and society is the process of contradiction, which in a generalized form consists in the fact that products of human social activity or labour confront the social actor as objective, external and constraining social phenomena independent of his own definition of the situation or his awareness of its contingencies. These slowly and collectively generate conditions of self-obsolescence and self-destruction of historically created social and cultural institutions and their replacement by new ones".[7]

As regards the capitalistic model of modernization, it is based upon capitalistic economy. It is obvious that the system of capitalism and capitalistic economy developed under the impact of mass production and industrialization of society. The technological achievements and the growth of many industries resulted in the accumulation of wealth by privileged sections of society and the owners of the production system. It is also obvious that this capitalistic economy developed first in USA and Western European countries because industrialization first started in the west. Modernization in Eastern Europe and America started with the growth of heavy industries. The system of capitalistic economy that the growth of industrialization has emphasised under this system and man is not considered as a species-man under Marxist ideology but as an individual. Thus, the concept of modernization under capitalistic ideology has a different root and is related to different suppositions. Yogendra Singh has explained the capitalistic model of modernization in a better way. Singh is of the view that "the capitalist ideology of modernization, which is not less differentiated internally than Marxism, is based on suppositions which are fundamentally different. Its paradigm is devoid of the notion of history and species character of man; the unit category in this sociology is not species man but 'individual'—who is an abstract rational being; the social system is a contrived reality, a matter of consensus among the rationally motivated individual members who comprise the society. The social system thus essentially pulls towards stability and equilibrium, and since the rationality is an integral component of societal consensus or its normative principles, 'growth' through innovations is assumed to be an ongoing and permanent feature of human societies. At the base of this growth is the rational urge for achievement and progressive well-being in the individual members of society. Innovative urges, to begin with, start as deviant tendencies, but in course of time their peripheral position becomes central through rationalization of the new innovation in the old system through adaptive transformation. Sometimes, in this ideological system, the individual as a category is replaced by categories that are more abstract, such as roles, functions, action systems, etc., for the formulation of the societal entities. These, however, perform the same heuristic function in constructing societal and cultural systems that are seen to be developing through stages of growth. Conflict does arise in this process, but all conflicts can be resolved without fundamentally altering the structure of society, provided the system has been able to enhance its *adaptive capacity*".[8]

The capitalist model of economic modernization is followed by models of political and cultural modernization, commensurate with its ideological ethos. It puts emphasis on the rational motivation of individuals by artificially detaching it from man's species condition and its historical contradictions; it frames the setting for modernization through rational adaptive transformations in societies, overlooking the contingency of 'encapsulation' of vital interests and ideas, which trigger the process of alienation of groups and classes in society and provide the framework for 'revolutionary *praxis*'. Finally, it formulates an ideology of 'consensus' or 'cooperation' between the 'centre' and the 'periphery' of social systems on economic and cultural issues which completely neglects the structure of 'dependency' that the processes of economic growth generate, in the words of sociologist Fernande Henrique Cordoso. This neglect follows from the detachment of 'economics' in the capitalist model of modernization from its political ideological implications. It overlooks the logical possibility that a certain rationality of the economic actions or choices in one context may well be concomitant with irrationality in political and cultural choices at another level or context of society.

Cordoso's thesis on 'dependency' of the nations at the periphery or in the Third World is in fact a reflection on the historical contradictions of the capitalist thesis on modernization through economic growth based on a false ideology of 'consensus' of interests between the rich nations and the poor. In fact, there exists a fundamental contradiction between the economic interests and ideology of the 'metropolitan' (rich, imperialist) nations in relation to those of the 'colonies'.[9]

Yogendra Singh has explained that "closely related to this 'dependency', theory which exposes the capitalist model of modernization is a Third World ideology of modernization which not only rejects the capitalist model but also looks at the Marxist model of modernization from a fresh perspective. The word capitalism itself is accorded in this ideological approach a new phenomenology and structure of meaning, invoking in this context the principles of 'alienation' and 'encapsulation' of labour in modes of production that are profit oriented, whether profit accrues to the individual entrepreneur or to the state. The structural dilemmas of private capitalism according to this ideology are not minimized only by replacing it by state capitalism, as in the socialist block countries, because in the relationship between man the producer and his product, there still stands the alienative process of denial and deprivation for marketable profit. The continuance of the profit motive through substitute institutions also renders the relationship between the 'socialist' developed societies and the developing societies of the Third World not less 'dependent' than with the advanced capitalist nations. Ironically, the foundation of this conceptual framework lies in Lenin's theory of *Imperialism as the Highest Stage of Capitalism* which proposed that as a logical and necessary corollary of the advancement of capitalism, colonial exploitation of less developed nations would take place not as a historical accident but as a 'systematic' need. This systematic need lies not merely in the search of raw materials but that of markets, engendering internal contradictions in capitalism through imperialistic adventurism. In the Third World intellectual circles, inspired by nationalist ideology on the one hand and varieties of innovative paradigms of Marxism, such as the Trotskyite, Maoist, New Left and others on the other, two major outcomes have emerged: first, there is a widespread rejection of the capitalist ideology of modernization, and secondly, there is a general impulse to follow a socialist path of development and modernization. The model of socialism resembles the Marxist ideology in a diffuse innovative sense. Very often, the projection of this ideology is cast into the local historical and cultural ethos. Its vivid examples can be seen in the formulation of socialist ideology in Vietnam, Tanzania, Mexico, and several other Latin American, Asian and African nations".[10]

Yogendra Singh has further explained that "modernization in the Third World nations is not only a means of economic and social development but also a process for the projection of their cultural self-consciousness and national identity. The ideology of modernization which appeals to these nations is sharpened by the sense of history, the background of colonialism and the constant threat of neo-colonialism. The capitalist ideology of modernization being devoid of the base in history, and being doubly vitiated by the role capitalism plays in the expansion of the 'metropolis' and the exploitation of the 'colonies', does not appeal to the intelligentsia and elite of these nations and is highly suspect. The Marxist ideology has comparatively greater appeal, but only in its reformulated and innovative form, a form which conforms with the national cultural ethos. Hence, Marxism as a modernization ideology in most Third World nations provides a canopy under which along with some of its essential principles, a lot of local cultural, symbolic and emotional urges could be sheltered for self-assertion of national identity".[11]

Capitalistic ideology views modernization not as a process in historical continuity but as a process contributing to the growth and development of individualism adaptive to capitalistic economy. Modernization is not only a process but also a concept associated with certain characteristic features.

Most approaches to modernization can be grouped into two broad categories: structural and evolutionary.[12] The structural approach is rather preponderant in social sciences. It seeks to analyse modernization with the help of selected social or normative variables. Such variables as 'social mobilization'[13] growth of 'communication' media exposure,[14] democratic political institutions and values,[15] morals and norms conducive to modernization,[16] technological and economic resources of society,[17] and initial conditions[18] of society with respect to the presence of cultural and structural autonomy[19] of parts within the social system have been taken into consideration. Modernization is supposed to follow as a result of the presence of these variables in the social system; their intensity and proportion would determine the nature and extent of modernization in specific situations.[20]

The evolutionary approach to modernization, on the other hand, is based on more systematic theoretical assumptions. It treats modernization as an evolutionary stage in the life of human society. There are, however, differences in formation of the process of evolution and its direction. Its methodological formulation may be either structural-functional[21] or dialectical.[22] Similarly, the direction of evolution may be either unilinear[23] or multilinear[24]. A major difference between dialectical (Marxist) and structural-functional evolutionary approaches to modernization is that the former treats 'breakdown' in the established political, economic and structural framework of a society as a necessary and inevitable condition for development towards modernization. Class struggle and its international form of struggle between the rich and the poor nations are here assumed as necessary processes for such evolutionary achievements. Modernization even as a concept is understood differently, its focus being on changes in stratification system, the system of property ownership and ownership of productive resources in a nation,[25] and not on psychological-normative variables like 'achievement orientation', 'psychic mobility' and 'rational hedonism', etc., common among the treatments of many social scientists. Individual characteristics are treated here as by-products of major aggregates of changes in institutional structure of society and its structure of power and property relationships.[26]

Structural breakdown in modernization, according to Parsons' theory, emerges when due to historical or other cultural factors, the sequence of evolution is reversed or made uneven or when some of the universals become far too rigid and offer more than normal resistance to further evolution. Such conditions, according to a later study by Buck and Jacobson, prevail in the Asian nations. These nations, being ex-colonies, have many evolutionary structures like bureaucracy, democratic associations and generalized universalistic norms introduced into their social structure without adequate development of other basic founding universals like communication, technology, stratification and principles of legitimation.[27] This is true of countries like Indonesia, India, Pakistan and many others in Africa, Latin America and the Middle East. Particularly about India, Buck and Jacobson's study reveals higher development in respect of bureaucracy and generalized universalistic norms but very poor growth in the spheres of communication, kinship, technology, social stratification and money and market complex.[28] Thus, value support to many modern institutions is lacking, and the wholesale transfer of many institutions from the west renders the lag more acute.[29]

There are many assumptions in Parsons' evolutionary theory of modernization which may not be accepted by other sociologists. For instance, his assertion that 'democratic association' is the highest evolutionary stage in the process of modernization, could be variously interpreted or even refuted both by Marxist and non-Marxist sociologists. Gunnar Myrdal writes: "Yet it may be doubted whether this ideal of political democracy with political power based on free elections and with freedom of assembly, press and other civil liberties—should be given weight in formulating the modernization ideals. This is not because the ideal is at present not very fully met, and may not be met in the future: value premises represent merely an angle from which actual conditions are viewed and need not be 'realistic' in that sense .... This democratic ideal is not essential to a system comprising all the other modernization ideals."[30]

Despite these limitations, which emanate from value premises of modernization, Parsons' formulation is theoretically powerful and could be used to explain many structural and cultural contradictions of modernization in underdeveloped countries. Stratification is one important factor which causes bottlenecks in the rapid modernization of India by its rigidity and non-egalitarian character. His model also delineates a course of modernization hypothetically, which would involve least conflict through stages of transition.[31]

In recent years, the term 'modernization' has come to be used with startling frequency to characterize this urge for change. Opinions as to what is implied by the word 'modernization' vary widely.[32]

David Apter's research on political development and change best illustrates the sociological approach. Apter has presented three models of the forms which the transitional political systems take.

The Mobilization Model

This is characterized by a single party dominance, and the regime "engages in drastic and thorough recognition of the society"[33] and has (i) a hierarchically structured authority system, (ii) 'total allegiance' to the party, (iii) a remarkable flexible party, (iv) a unitary party, opposed to any other groups or organization other than itself, and (v) 'ideological specialization'.[34] Ideology is used to support the actions of the regimes.

The Consociational Model

Under this model (i) the authority is 'pyramidal'; it is not concentrated at the centre but is dispersed among constituent subordinate units; (ii) 'tolerance of multiple loyalties'; individuals are not expected to commit themselves totally to one leader or any party; they may belong to other parties or groups; (iii) the social order is 'pluralistic', hence diverse and competing political and social 'sub-groups' exist; and (iv) there is 'ideological diffuseness'. The constituent units are held together by ideology. The alliance or union between these groups is not merely based on 'necessity for compromise'.

The Modernizing Autocracy Model

Under this model, social and political change can be generated by the traditional system of authority. Here: (i) The authority is hierarchical, and is not vested in one particular leader himself but in the leadership role. (ii) The principle of 'exclusiveness' is found in this model. "To belong means not to belong to another social grouping of a similar nature and not to divide one's fundamental allegiance, however, persons can belong to a range of voluntary associations and political groups". (iii) There is 'strategic flexibility' which provides freedom to develop long term plans. (iv) The organizational structure is 'unitary'. (v) The model tends to have 'neotraditional' ideology.[35] One of the significant contributions of Apter's work is a theory that explains why one rather than another of these systems develops (or will develop) during the transitional stage of political development.

Apter holds that instrumental values are a very important and essential part of a modern system, and modernization could be introduced without discarding the basis of legitimacy of the traditional authority and system. It is through the fusion of traditional and modern systems that traditional autocracy can become a modernizing autocracy. In Apter's conceptualization, all the variables are social system variables. But, this does not mean that he rejects the important role of psychological variables in political development and change. Apter's conceptualization has been presented by Holt and Turner in the following scheme:[36]

Independent variable	intervening variable (traditional system)	dependent variable (traditional type)
	pyramidal, consummatory →	mobilized system
Colonial impact <		
	hierarchical, instrumental → traditional system	modernizing autocracy

The Psychological Model

'Modernity' is 'primarily a state of mind'. It is 'psychic mobility'. There is a close relationship between 'self-awareness' and change. The attributes of self-awareness .. are central to our understanding of the pre-requisites of man's social and cultural mode of adjustment as it is for the psychodynamics of the individual ... An organized social life in man, since it transcends purely biological and geographical determinants, cannot function apart from communally recognized meanings and values.[37]

Pye, in his study, *Politics, Personality and Nation Building*, has presented a theoretical framework providing psychological explanations of social system phenomena. He is primarily interested in the role of personality factors in nation building and political development. He feels that "it will be helpful to elucidate the details of relationships between personality and social change".[38] An analysis of various phases of political socialization processes, and their 'significance for social change', is recommended. Pye found that because of the Burmese administrator's socialization experiences, he is insecure and distrustful and has failed to develop associational sentiments, and therefore, a modern society cannot develop when the crucial large-scale organizations have disproportionate number of insecure and distrustful individuals in them. Pye also discovered that there is a high incidence of acts of violence in Burmese society due to a 'deep-seated fear of provoking others'. He observes: "..when people are being changed from traditionals into moderns, they are likely to be hypersensitive to the deeply felt sensation of being changed and manipulated by others who always protest that they are only being helpful.[39]

McClelland sought to show that an essential ingredient of entrepreneurship leading to economic development is achievement development motivation. McClelland is of the view that achievement motivation is a social value that emphasizes a desire for excellence in order to obtain a sense of personal accomplishment. The central social value in McClelland's model—achievement motivation is not specially defined, but he equates it to an inner concern with achievement, a disposition to engage in activities in which doing well or competing with a standard of excellence is important. The similarity between achievement motivation and certain aspects of the Protestant Ethic is noted by McClelland.

Certainly, Weber's description of the kind of personality type which the Protestant reformation produces is startlingly similar to the picture we have drawn of a person with high achievement motivation.[40]

McClelland's basic research design delineating his pattern of personality change has been presented in the following way by Alfred Diamant:[41]

Value associated with modern industrialism		Entrepreneurship
v		v
Independence and mastery training	→	Achievement

McClelland has been able to show how the values associated with modern industrialism produced child-rearing patterns which led the parents to encourage in the child early (but not too early) independence and the habit of doing things for himself (mastery training). It is these practices that are associated with a high achievement motive (n achievement), which in turn McClelland links with entrepreneurship. McClelland leaves no doubt that the crucial variable which spurs individuals to foster economic development is not profit, but achievement.

Historical Models

S.N. Eisenstadt, Harold Isaac, Myron Winer, Robert Wood, Talcott Parsons, Robert N. Bellah and Edward Shils have presented historical models. They have provided the crucial concepts of the 'consensual mass society' and 'centre and periphery'.[42]

In India, current conceptualizations of the process of modernization fall into two broad categories:[43]

Historically-Oriented Formulations

Despite important differences in approach, method and rigour, historically-oriented studies share certain common features, the most notable of which are a scepticism of overly rigorous analytic frame, greater reliance on ad hoc imagination and judgement in discerning general trends, and a desire to keep to the main factual terrain as defined by their focus of study. These studies have contributed towards an understanding, interpretation or explanation of the complex ongoing processes of social change, as seen in the historical perspective. However, their significance is rather limited due to their thin theoretical fall-out. They fail to undertake an empirical exploration of the contemporary situation or attempt a prediction of emerging trends.[44]

Analytically-Oriented Formulations

The studies under this category adopt an analytic approach, and try not only to explain the process of modernization but also to predict the trends. One of the efforts in this regard was pioneered by S.C. Dube. Modernity, for Dube[45], denotes the common 'behavioural systems' historically associated with the urban, industrial, literate and participant societies of Western Europe and North America as well as those of USSR and Japan. Modernization is the process through which their standards of performance and achievement can be accomplished by the less developed societies.

Modernization involves the emergence of a new behavioural system with certain distinctive characteristics. Such a system implies considerable value-change. Unless the traditional values undergo a radical modification, an innovative ethos and an entrepreneurial and an industrial ethic cannot be created. Value-change is necessary also for institutional rearrangement considered essential for modernization.[46]

Modernity, thus, is not just superficial acquisition of some isolated traits and elements characteristic of the more advanced countries. Their selection in a logical order and sequence, and integration into the cultural pattern in a widely ramifying manner is essential.[47]

In offering his own model, Dube draws from the works of Lerner (Rogers and Svenning have presented Lerner's model in 'symbolic' notation as:

Urbanization→ Literacy→ Mass Media Exposure→ Income and Voting).

According to the Almond-Coleman model, structure differentiation exists when there are structures in the political systems that have a "functional distinctiveness, and which tend to perform ... a regulatory role in relation to that function within the political system as a whole". To have a meaningful understanding of structural differentiation it seems necessary to identify the functions that all political systems have in common. These functions are classified into two main categories: (i) input functions, and (ii) output functions. The input functions are: (a) political socialization and recruitment, (b) interest articulation, (c) interest aggregation, and (d) political communication. The output functions are: (a) rule-making, (b) rule application, and (c) rule adjudication. A differentiated political system has specialized in each of these functional areas. Almond and Coleman do not offer a precise and detailed definition and mention it very briefly. In short, the Almond and Coleman model of the modern political system is structurally differentiated and secular and is a system in which the input functions are performed in a specified style.[48] McClelland lists the characteristic attributes of modernity as under:

1. Empathy
2. Mobility
3. High participation
4. Interest articulation
5. Interest aggregation
6. Institutionalized political competition
7. Achievement orientation
8. Rational ends—means calculation
9. New attitudes to wealth, work, savings, and risk-taking
10. Faith in the desirability and possibility of change
11. Social, economic, and political discipline
12. Capacity to put off immediate and short-term satisfactions for higher satisfactions in the long run

As is apparent, the first three attributes are components of the Lerner model; the next three are adoptions from the Almond-Coleman model; the seventh attribute comes from McClelland; while the last five relate to attitudes, values and motivations—articulated in the growing literature on social and cultural implications of modernization, more especially by Ithiel de Sola Pool, Wilbert Moore and S.C. Dube. The author recognizes the importance of the sequence or specific form of linkage between the items listed.[49]

Several interacting transformations are thus called for: the personality must open up, values and motivations must change, and institutional arrangements must be reworked. An integrated combination of these attributes leads to modernization.[50]

The critical question as to the specific mode of 'integrated combination', however, is left unanswered. Dube comments: "The requirements of modernization are hard and almost inflexible. They will not yield, beyond a point, to particular societies. Societies must yield to them. The dialogue on their adaptive demands on Indian society has so far yielded only polite nothings. Fashionable debates on the subject diplomatically avoid facing the real issues. It is necessary that they be faced with candour and conviction."[51]

These changes occur both at the individual (micro) and social system (macro) levels, and these two levels are not mutually exclusive. The modernization process is not unidimensional and, therefore, cannot be measured by a single index.[52]

Tradition and Modernity

According to Yogendra Singh, "tradition and modernity as heuristic concepts are easy to formulate, but to separate them at substantive level is rather difficult". As Joseph R. Gusfield has said: "We cannot easily separate modernity and tradition from some *specific* modernity, some version which functions ideologically as a directive. The modern comes to the traditional society as a particular culture with its own traditions." But it seldom comes in the same form or brings about identical cultural consequences in every society that it comes in contact with. Modernization, as a process, in fact, has more elasticity of form than tradition. It implies an open worldview which like science undergoes perpetual self-falsification and self-transcendence in its value-structure and postulates.

Comparative studies on modernization in the new states have shown that contrary to stereotyped beliefs, old traditions are not completely displaced by modernization: what follows is an accretion and transmutation of forms. Similarly, tradition does not necessarily retard the process of modernization. As we have mentioned above, religious leaders in Indonesia studied by Geertz serve as carriers of modernization. In India, caste associations, which are otherwise typical symbols of tradition, have increasingly been found to serve the ends of political modernization. Lloyd I. Rudolph calls this phenomenon 'modernity of tradition' and concludes with Edward Shils that "modernity has entered into Indian character and society but it has done so through assimilation and not replacement". Other studies in Indian social processes also provide evidence that traditional institutions like the joint family, and kin-based entrepreneurial functions continue to co-exist with and support modern values and forms of social action. From the advancement in modern means of transport and communication not only the cultural diffusion of modernization but also that of traditionalism is accelerated.

These processes in the institutional realm of modernization are also in harmony with the historical growth of this phenomenon in India. Historically as we discussed above, the rise of the nationalistic movement which later changed into a movement for political, cultural and economic modernization was itself never bereft of the consciousness of the past tradition of India. The new leadership that is now emerging is more conscious of national identity and prides in the traditional culture of India. Consequently, it is fair to assume that the forces of cultural modernization growing there will also simultaneously grow the feeling of national identity and the identification with the nation's past tradition. Cultural modernization will, under this process, assume a syncretic form and persist along with traditional values. Modernity will never completely supplant tradition in India."[53]

The traditional approach to the study of modernization has been to consider tradition and modernity as polar opposites, and exclusive. The more you have one, the less you have the other. Modernity and tradition, according to this view, are dichotomous. In this approach, the basic assumption is that the social structures of traditional societies are simple, homogeneous, static, particularistic, closed, dominated by customs and age-old traditions. These societies are less differentiated—with a primitive agrarian economy, and ascriptive system. 'Modernity', contrary to the traditional model, represents rationality, emphasis on achievement, a complex social structure, industrial urbanism, and an elaborate institutional framework. It has a 'rationalist and positivist spirit'.[54] Rostow thinks that the traditional societies are dominated by kinship and lack certain preconditions of science and technology. Their economy depends mainly on agriculture, which often suffers from fluctuations depending on the natural conditions. According to Rostow, "modernization starts with the 'take off' which is the 'break' from tradition".[55]

In any society, the property to generate changes and also to some extent absorb them is built into the traditional structure of the modern social system. The same is true at the level of values. We are so attuned to the idea of contradiction between modernization and the religious worldview that whenever we find evidence of modernity, we look for, or tend to expect, those social and political changes which we are accustomed to find associated with modernity. In fact, modernization is not in conflict with religious or traditional values.

It is possible to define modernization in a way which is not committed to this bi-polar viewpoint. It could be formulated at two levels as suggested by Bellah: as a system of new role structures, meaning thereby a network of roles, contingent modern skills and values, and as a dual system of values, the first one being basic to a scientific worldview which lies in a scientific evaluational approach to the normative problems of human life and is open-ended, continuously revisable, and relativistic; the second value system, however, refers to the categorical values free from the instrumental definition of science, being rooted in the wider existential reality of man.[56]

A realistic formulation of modernization should describe this process in terms of role structure emerging from the continual impingement of science and technology, and continual differentiation of social structure on the social system, a system of values representing a scientific worldview, and a parallel system of values categorical in nature and representing both a self-transcendence of pre-existing traditions as well as the traditions of modern science. And, a formulation may be free from the fallacies of unilinear ethnocentrism that most formulations of modernization empty.

An important question about modernization is regarding the direction in which the process takes societies. In this connection, there are various formulations.[57] One important view treats modernization as a unilinear evolutionary process whose growth would bring all societies to a level of cultural identities. Following from this logic, such writers also treat modernization as equivalent to westernization. Modernization is thought of as a process of confrontation between the western and non-western societies with the help of technological and scientific symbolism now rather than of Christianity as in the past.

In such formulations a universal stage of a conflict between the native traditions and modernity is also postulated. Toynbee mentions in this connection, traditional China's resistance to the west, xenophobia during the Tukogava regime in Japan and the efforts of Mahatma Gandhi in India to offer alternative solutions to modernization. In all these societies, however, these efforts finally failed under the impact of westernization.[58]

The quintessence of Toynbee's treatment of modernization is based on the assumption that westernization is equivalent to modernization. Obviously, his concept suffers from the fallacy of historicism. The formulation of modernization is entirely based on its first two attributes, namely the role structure and the value system of science. It neglects the role of categorical values in modernization.[59]

Process of Modernization

According to Yogendra Singh,[60] "modernization in India started mainly with the western contact, especially through establishment of the British rule. This contact had a special historicity which brought about many far-reaching changes in culture and social structure of the Indian society. Not all of them, however, could be called modernizing. The basic direction of this contact was towards modernization, but in the process a variety of traditional institutions also got reinforcement. This demonstrates the weakness of assuming a neat contrariety between tradition and modernity. This polarity may be more heuristic than real. However, only after the establishment of British rule in India modern cultural institutions and forms of social structure were introduced. In this respect the impact of Western tradition fundamentally differed from that of Islam, although both were heterogenetic and both began with political domination and rulership. The Western tradition at the time of contact had itself undergone fundamental transformations through Industrial Revolution and social reformation. Its traditional principle of hierarchy in stratification represented both by Church and feudalism were shaken; its medieval holism of value system was seriously jeopardized by the emergence of Protestantism, and was on the way out. Its place was now being taken by rational-individualism in economy and society. The basic dynamism to all these processes was imparted by a cumulative chain of innovations in science and technology. It was a period of extreme optimism and ever more accelerated rate of social change in the West, particularly Britain.

'The social background to a large extent determined the attitude of the British rulers and administrators about modernization in India; another determining factor was their colonial status. With the exception of a handful of Orientalists who were overwhelmed by the textual grandeur of Indian tradition, the majority of British missionaries and administrators were only impressed by contrasts which Indian society presented to their own Western society'. 'Indian society appeared to them as consisting of discrete plural traditions of castes, sub-castes and tribes devoid of a systematic binding force of a universal nature. The significance of British contribution to modernization mainly lies in the creation of such networks of social structure and culture which were modern and pan-Indian'.

Initially, the contact led to the growth of a modernizing sub-culture or a little tradition of Westernization, especially during the seventeenth century in Bengal, Madras and Bombay, where emerged a small nucleus of interpreters, trader-cum-middlemen emerged who were slowly being socialized to Western ways; subsequently, there also emerged sects which emphasized assimilation of Western cultural norms, and Western modes of learning (e.g., Brahmo Samaj, Prarthana Samaj, etc.); these also ran a crusade against obscurantism in Hindu traditions. These movements on the one hand and the consolidation of the British power towards the middle of the nineteenth century on the other, finally led to the institution of a modernizing great tradition. Its components were: a universalistic legal system, expansion of Western form of education, urbanization and industrialization, spread of new means of communication and transport and social reforms. Along with these modernization norms structural modernization also took place. For instance, rational bureaucratic systems of administration and judiciary, army, and industrial bureaucracy, new classes of business elite and entrepreneurs came into being. These were accompanied by the emergence of political elite and a nationalist leadership by the middle of the nineteenth century. Growth of an industrial entrepreneurship also contributed to the emergence of industrial working class and trade unions organized on corporate lines as in the West. These modernizing structures had a uniform character throughout the country. Their development led, therefore, to articulation of nationalist aspirations in the country which itself was a major step in the growth of modernization.

There was, however, one important feature of Indian modernization during the British period. The growth of this process was selective and segmental. It was not integrated with the micro-structures of Indian society, such as family, caste and village community. At these levels, the British by and large followed a policy of least interference, especially after the rebellion of 1857. Moreover, some British administrators were wrongly impressed by the staticness and autonomy of these micro-structures compared with the rest of the Indian society. This was especially so about the notion of village community, and importance attributed to caste. For a long time caste and ethnic factors were given recognition in recruitment of officers to army and middle and lower ranks of bureaucracy. Later, in the twentieth century, as the nationalist movement gathered momentum, a communal electorate system was introduced. These historical factors have deeply influenced the process of modernization which followed during the post-colonial period. It increased the contingency of traditional institutions and symbolisms to the Indian process of modernization.

This development is fully articulated in the freedom movement and the pace of modernization of Indian society thereafter. Freedom movement ushered in a new political culture of modernization. At its centre was the personality of Mahatma Gandhi whose one foot was always deeply embedded in tradition. His emergence during the peak of the

Westernization process in India signifies an orthogenetic response of Indian tradition to the new challenges of social change. Gandhi successfully mobilized Indian people for the attainment of freedom, but he could not, however, avert one serious breakdown in this process ... the partition of India into two independent nations. As we mentioned above, it followed from the uneven growth of sub-cultural traditions of modernization in Hinduism and Islam, each conditioned by unique historicity of their own. The quest for a separate nationhood by the Muslim community in India reflected a crisis of aspiration along with that of confidence.

Following independence, the modernization process in India has undergone a basic change from its colonial pattern. As an integral part of developmental strategy, now modernization has been envisaged at all levels of cultural and structural systems. Discontinuity in modernization between macro-structures and micro-structures and between the little and great traditions, as during the British regime, has now been consciously abolished. Introduction of adult suffrage and a federal parliamentary form of political structure have carried politicization to every sector of social organization. Conscious legal reforms in Hindu marriage and inheritance laws have deeply affected the foundations of traditional Hindu family structure. Community Development Projects have carried the cultural norms and role-structures of modernity to each and every village in India, and this, coupled with introduction of land reforms and elective village panchayats, has initiated villagers to a bureaucratic form of participation in local level management and administration of justice. Caste has, in the process, undergone radical transformation of roles, developed new functional adaptations and activated aspirations unleashed by democratization of polity and power structure. We have analysed in detail how caste is increasingly developing an associational character. Now, it functions as an important structural network in the process of modernization.

As the process of modernization becomes all encompassing, it also generates inter-structural tensions and conflicts between traditions (past and contemporary). Future course of modernization in India would depend much on the manner in which these tensions are resolved as modernization gathers momentum. In many developing countries in Asia, modernization contributed to a structural and cultural breakdown in society. The cases of China, Indonesia, Burma and Pakistan could be cited. The only successful case of modernization in Asia is that of Japan, but there too its institutionalization has not been without a breakdown following the Second World War."

Institutionalization and Breakdown in Modernization: The Indian Scene

Yogendra Singh[61] has explained that "modernization, in its initial stage in India, according to Eisenstadt, did not lead to any serious breakdown because of the peculiar structural characteristics of the Indian society. Here, cultural system was fairly independent of political system". Louis Dumont writes: "This domain (polity or artha) is, in the dominant tradition, relatively autonomous with regard to absolute values." There was also independence between the political system and the system of caste stratification. Castes had their own panchayats and plural traditions, and similarly there also existed an autonomy for groups and regional communities. This inter-structural autonomy facilitated assimilation of modernizing innovations, without introducing any major breakdown. Modernity, however, mainly developed as a sub-structure and sub-culture without pervasive expansion in all sectors of life.

The colonial phase of modernization did not seriously articulate many structural challenges which now the totalization of this process in free India implies. As the segmental nature of modernization becomes encompassing, relevance of structural autonomy ceases to operate as a shock-absorber. Changes in political system begin increasingly to impinge upon the system of stratification (caste, class, ethnic communities), and these together create serious stresses for the cultural system as a whole. The cultural pre-requisites of a comprehensive modernization necessitate adaptive changes in the system of values which come in direct confrontation with traditional cultural values and norms. For instance, secularism, untouchability, non-parochialism are some cultural demands of modernization in contemporary India which its traditional value system continues to resist. The question thus arises: Will Indian society be able to avoid structural breakdown also in the second phase of modernization? Will not the advantage which it formerly enjoyed through structural autonomy, become, under the changed circumstances, a bottleneck for smooth institutionalization of modernity?

The answer to these questions can be formulated only through objective analysis of important trends of social and cultural changes in India which are relevant to the process of modernization. In the cultural sphere, major changes have been introduced by legislations. These seek to abolish social inequalities and exploitations handed down by tradition and accord democratic rights and constitutional privileges to all members of society. This has led to a trend away from Sanskritization (emulation of the great tradition) and towards formation of new identities and associations of castes, regional groups and tribes. These processes are accelerated by 'great traditions' of modernization such as, urbanization, industrialization, spread of education, and politicization. The traditional structures and loyalties are being mobilized for objectives which are essentially modern and there is an increased emphasis on protest movements. However, the tradition also gets reinforcement in the process; modern media of communication and transport are increasingly used for spreading ritual order and for rational organization of religious groups and their mode of activities and social participation. There is a tendency among religious sects to organize themselves on a rational bureaucratic model, and the previous fission of each new sect from the parent body has now changed into strong orientation towards fusion.

Inconsistencies are similarly there in structural changes that India has undergone during the post-colonial phase of modernization. Micro-structures like caste, family and village community have retained their traditional character; caste has shown unexpected elasticity and latent potential for adaptation with modern institutions, such as democratic participation, political party organization and trade unionism, and it persists unabatedly. Joint family loyalties and particularistic norms continue to prevail. These contradictions are, however, further magnified at the level of macro-structures, such as the political system, bureaucracy, elite structure, industry and economy. The colonial period of modernization had a homogeneity in elite structure. These elite from industrial, civil and military bureaucracies, as well as political spheres came from similar class-caste stratum; they had an equitable exposure to western education, and socialization. They also had uniformity of ideologies and aspirations. This was because the social base for recruitment of these elite was limited. This has fairly widened during the post-independence period; it may not be equitable in terms of stratification system, but in cultural background there is enough representativeness which leads to many contradictions. A gap is specially coming into being between political elite and non-political elite; the former are less Westernized, and externally at least identify with traditional cultural symbolisms more strongly than the latter. Contradictions are also growing in the federal structure of the Union as one party government is being replaced by multi-party governments in states, having divergent ideological policies (Communist-led united fronts in Kerala and West Bengal, D.M.K. in Tamil Nadu). There is also evidence that, in the course of three Five-Year Plans additional income generated by economic investments has gone in favour of only the well-to-do classes to the determent of poorer sections. Planning has thus accentuated and sharpened the gaps in social stratification. This along with the slow rate of economic growth and rapid increase in population creates additional intensities for structural tensions. Despite the years of effort at industrialization, India continues to be a rural-peasant dominated society with general poverty of living standards.

Thus, major potential sources of breakdown in the Indian process of modernization may, in one form or another, be attributed to structural inconsistencies, such as: democratization without spread of civic culture (education), bureaucratization without commitment to universalistic norms, rise in media participation (communication) and aspiration without proportionate increase in resources and distributive justice, verbalization of a welfare ideology without its diffusion in social structure and its implementation as a social policy, over-urbanization without industrialization and finally modernization without meaningful changes in the stratification system.

Gunnar Myrdal refers to similar impediments to modernization in India and other Asian countries in his work *Asian Drama*. Nationalism and democratic institutions themselves, according to him, have grown in a structurally uneven form in these countries. "In Europe, strong independent state with a fairly effective government and a common pattern of law enforcement," he says, "preceded nationalism, and both preceded democracy"; in South Asian countries democratic ideology if not reality, has, due to special historicity, preceded strong and independent State and effective government, and this is further complicated by onslaught of nationalism. This uneven historicity goes along with economic dependence of these countries on developed nations and slow rate of economic growth and still slower pace of institutional changes. Particularly in India, which, according to Myrdal, has a more viable size of intellectuals and middle classes necessary for democracy, planned economic growth has not made as deep an impact towards liberalizing the structural bottlenecks for modernization as should have been expected. According to Myrdal,

India's 'soft-state' policy after independence inhibited its leadership from going to the root of the problem, that is, introduction of basic changes in the institutional structure of society. Consequently, the inegalitarian structure of society continued to grow and consolidate itself; there developed a long gap between verbalization (even enactment) and implementation of policies of reform; the decentralization of power in rural sectors led to concentration of power in the hands of a petty plutocracy. Also the leadership of the country as a whole remained with those who are opponents of real economic and social change.

Myrdal's well-known position on theory of social change and development is that of circular causation and cumulative change. He suspects the validity of constructing universal evolutionary stages of 'growth'. These according to him tend to be teleological and often have conservative ideologies latent in them. The crucial factor in development is an 'upward' movement of the social system as a whole with all its component 'conditions'. These conditions for South Asian countries as described by Myrdal are: (1) output and income; (2) conditions of production; (3) levels of living; (4) attitudes towards life and work; (5) institutions; and (6) policies. He assumes a uni-directional causal relationship between these conditions; an 'upward' or 'downward' movement in one would cause cumulative movement of similar nature in other conditions too. Value premises related to these conditions might differ from country to country, specially in regard to conditions which are treated for their 'independent' (as a goal in themselves) values as different from those having 'instrumental' values. These valuations define ideological contexts of development in each national society, but their selectivity is organically linked with attributes of social system as a whole. The modernization process in India and other South Asian countries, according to Myrdal, is heading fast towards a climax, and the time for reasonable choice for them is limited. The opportunity for a 'gradualist' approach is also over.

Myrdal thinks that "it is not more difficult, but easier, to cause a big change rapidly than a small change gradually. The prime areas for such big, rapid changes are social and institutional conditions in Indian society. These conditions (4 and 5 of the above) hold the keys for the mobilization of all other conditions of development".

Myrdal's theory of modernization could best be evaluated through the distinction he introduces between 'independent' and 'instrumental' values that institutions and social realities of a society ('conditions') have for their people. The 'independent values' of a traditional society differ from those of a modern society, and more often they are mutually contradictory. But the 'independent values' cannot be demonstrated to be false or irrelevant without transforming them into 'instrumental values'. Since, the institutions and attitudes towards life and work in a traditional society came to be valued for their 'independent values', it is necessary to demonstrate their poverty over 'independent values' of a modern society in order to motivate people to renounce them for the latter. This, however, cannot be realized without introducing the medium of 'instrumental values'. If we want to convince people that "(A) a closed system of stratification is bad" and "(B) an open system of stratification is good", then we have to demonstrate also that "(C) the goal of social justice cannot be realized in a closed stratification system, but can be easily accomplished in an open system." People would change their independent value (A) for (B), more easily when the instrumental value (C) they cherish, is shown to have closer association with the latter (B) than the former (A).

As we have explained above, the crucial variable to bring this about lies in mobilization of people's motivations for change on utilitarian grounds or what Myrdal calls the grounds of rationality. If we accept this, then it would appear that Myrdal's overemphasis on priority of radical changes first in the value systems of the developing society over the more instrumental or structural 'conditions' such as income, production, etc., tend to be highly unrealistic. To our mind it is difficult to begin with radical value changes in traditional society in order to facilitate the growth of modern instrumental structures. In fact, Myrdal votes for a 'mobilization system' of social transformation which is valid but does not logically conform with his emphasis on first changing the values or institutions rather than the structures of society.

The institutional changes are, however, necessary for coordinating modernizing changes in other structural conditions of a society, but no general hypothesis, that a 'big-push' policy of change in institutions is preferable to a 'gradualist' approach to change, can be tenable. This in fact, contradicts Myrdal's own theory of balance among various 'conditions' for development and modernization. The more important factor will be rational coordination rather than the 'big-push' policy which in an uncoordinated manner might inevitably contribute to a breakdown in the social structure, especially in India where democratic polity and way of life have been accepted as independent values.

In fact, the emergent tensions caused by processes of modernization in India do direct our attention to much needed further coordination in the strategy of change with radical changes in policy. Contradictions are emerging in the system at various points as a result of uncoordinated institutional reforms and economic measures introduced for modernization during the post-independence period. These contradictions, however, also inhere in and symbolize the frictions caused by upward movement of hitherto suppressed aspirations and interests of groups. Protest movements, whether disguised (like Sanskritization, Islamization, formation of parochial associations based on caste, language and regional culture) or overt (centre-state tensions) are inevitable in democratic transition to modernization. These, of course, indicate the specific areas where institutional and other reforms could further be accelerated to remove friction in the process of change. Modernization should thus proceed by a series of conciliatory steps through a forceful strategy of mobilization in the course of the developmental process. The need is also simultaneously to reinforce the democratic values and institutions. Given a democratic political framework, there exists a built-in mechanism in this system to build pressures for removal of inconsistencies emerging from uncoordinated changes in the 'conditions' of modernization; but the same cannot be said to be true for other forms of totalitarian political systems.

On the Indian scene it appears that, despite continual tensions and contradictions, chances of institutional breakdown are minimal; democratic values have fairly institutionalized in the political system; cultural gap which has recently widened between various levels of the elite does not go far enough to introduce major conflict about the ideology of modernization. Caste, which represents an institutionalized form of inequality sanctioned by tradition now fights battles against inequality and inegalitarianism by its own rational self-transformation into associations; many independent or categorical values of tradition have shown a surprising degree of elasticity to adapt themselves to the cultural system of modernization. Some of these traditions even thrive as modernization processes accelerate without creating major contradictions. In the realm of material resources too, the recent 'agricultural revolution' in the countryside has created a new atmosphere of optimism for future progress. This, along with people's increasing awareness to curb the birth rate may point towards new hopeful signs of modernization without a breakdown.

This assumption would, however, rest on one major conditional assumption, that at no stage in the Indian process of development would conciliation as a goal of resolving contradictions be renounced or replaced by a policy of controlled suppression. A constant coordination of mobilization with conciliation is a pre-requisite for democratic form of modernization in India."

Historicity of Modernization

Yogendra Singh states that "The problems connected with historicity of modernization emerge from the 'initial conditions' of different societies from where modernization as a process starts. The differences in these conditions may be both cultural and social structural in origin and lead to variations in adaptive patterns in modernization, which have been recognized by many social scientists. In contrast with evolutionary universalistic theory of modernization these social scientists hold that modernization would develop typical forms in different societies. This is also our contention in this essay.

There are both logical and substantive grounds why growth of modernization might vary in pattern from society to society. Often, modernization is defined through attributes which are too abstract and partial in nature and do not take account of the dynamics of social and cultural forces in each society. Modernization is understood as growth of a uniform set of cultural and role-structural attributes, but attention is not paid as to how these attributes develop typical adaptations within the traditional conditions of each society. This limitation, in our view, can be avoided if we conceptualize both tradition and modernization as sets of values and role-structures which interact as they come into contact, and between them a selective process of assimilation and syncretism starts. The crucial role in selective acceptance is played by the system of values. These values in each society are differentiated into (1) categorical or independent; and (2) instrumental types. All role-structures whether traditional or modern inhere both categorical and instrumental standards, and this leads to a combination of both; a person who is well-trained in the modern role-structure with high instrumental value, for instance, a surgeon or an engineer or a scientist, may be deeply committed to traditional categorical values. This is logically quite possible because the categorical values enjoy autonomy over the instrumental values. Such instances are quite common in Indian society, but it is presumed that no society would be an exception to this rule.

As for modernization in India, we find a growing trend that traditional role-structures are giving way to modern ones. But persons following these roles often retain categorical values of tradition instead of those of modernity. We have mentioned how caste itself is adopting many functions which properly belong to rational corporate groups. Generally, ritual order and religion which are essentially based on categorical values of a traditional nature do not show evidence of decline, nor is there an easy possibility of their disappearance in the near future. Since many of these categorical values differ from one society to another, there may always be a possibility of unique combination of traditional values with modern ones; the categorical values can hardly be falsified by scientific proof and hence the spread of science may not *logically* lead to obsolescence of traditional categorical values.

This would explain the diversity in the pattern of modernization in different societies. But it would be wrong to deduce from this argument that modernization will not bring about structural and cultural similarity among the peoples of the world. As modernization proceeds, it would create uniform sets of role-structures with accompanying modern value commitments, instrumental or categorical. Inconsistent combinations of roles and values may still persist but a large sector of societal and cultural life of societies would share uniformity of standards with other modern societies. Diversity may persist within this strong sense of unity in the traditions of mankind. The major factor would here be the nature of value premises that societies adopt for modernization. So far, however, no uniformity of such value premises is in sight. The divergence of political ideologies, contradictions in cultural and racial identities coupled with inequality of resources among nations create basic schism in the value-structure of modernization. Hence, particularistic growth pattern of modernization seems to be more credible than the universalistic form of its development."[62]

Challenges of Post-Modernity

In this concern, Yogendra Singh has analysed worldview of sociology and the challenges of post-modernity. According to Singh[63], "Fredric Jameson mentions two important features of post-modernism: first, 'transformation of reality into images' and secondly, 'fragmentation of time into a series of perpetual presents'. The birth of post-modernism, he says, could be traced to the 1960's, when "the position of high modernism and its dominant aesthetics become established in the academy and are henceforth felt to be academic by a whole new generation of poets, painters and musicians". It is no doubt the product of a social condition of late consumer and multinational capitalism riding the tide of the media-technology revolution. Its celebration of the 'present' and the 'instant' adds up to the 'disappearance of the sense of history' and the 'inability to retain the past' as it applauds 'perpetual change'. It seeks to efface linkages with tradition which most earlier social formations had. Post-modernism presents an epistemology which abolishes the role of normal language, language of speech and eschews most linguistic norms. It celebrates 'pastiche' instead of parody, a neutral practice of mimicry of style, which as Jameson (in Kaplan, 1988) writes, is "without that still latent feeling that there exists something *normal* compared to which what is being imitated is rather comic".

A more serious discourse on post-modernism is witnessed in the philosophical contributions of Jacques Derrida and its social science interface in the writings of Michel Foucault, Jean Baudrillard, Jacques Lacan, etc. Derrida, amongst them, is in the forefront in contributing to an epistemological-ontological perspective of post-modern philosophy. Language or text forms its point of beginning, 'differance' or 'difference' its elemental structure, through which Derrida weaves an epistemology of multidirectional usages of text and meanings. In his, *The Margin of Philosophy*, he uses the metaphor of a sheaf, since "the word sheaf seems to mark more appropriately that the assemblage (of the text) to be proposed has the complex structure of a weaving, an interlacing which permits different threads and different lines of meaning—or of force—to go off again in different directions, just as it is always ready to tie itself up with others". He is able to integrate in his notion of 'differance' the Freudian distinction between the 'pleasure principle' and the 'reality principle' innovatively used by Lacan, as also the notion of 'force' basic to Foucault's archeology of knowledge. Here, as also in the artistic style, the projected image of being and substance, whether ontological or epistemological, is that of impermanence or flux.

No doubt, post-modernism manifested itself first in the domain of art, literary styles and philosophical discourses. Its impact on the social sciences spread out slowly as sociologists increasingly had to cope up with the emergence of new social and cultural movements and institutional practices, which gained momentum from 1960's onwards. This was manifested in student movements, their disenchantment with consumerism sponsored by post-modern capitalism and supported by state, by a revolution in sexual mores, new awareness about gender issues and its ideology, multiculturalism and movements for ecological protection from mindless and self-centred industrialization. The post-modern challenge to sociology has its root in the post-modern social conditions. There seems to exist a clear relationship between philosophical articulation of post-modernity and the social changes that took place in society in its post-industrial phase.

Some of its obvious indicators are: the breakdown of community values and its structures due to high levels of social and psychological mobility of members in society; the revolutionary changes in the gender relationship and emergence of new family norms about marriage, childcare and conjugal responsibilities; and erosion in the participatory behaviour of individuals in the affairs of society and community, due to legitimization of self-referentiality in individual ethic. Alienation and anomie, which classical sociology held as problems created by the industrial society cease to be so perceived in the post-modern society. On the contrary, the borderline between freedom and alienation is so narrowed as to render the distinction infructuous. Mass media hyperconsumerism and the supremacy of images over values downgrade the role of the subject in the manifestation of post-modernity. David Reismann's paradox, of the 'lonely crowd', ceases to be a problem. It is legitimated or even applauded.

The post-modern society also brings about radical changes in the infrastructure of the economy. If the industrial-capitalism, which inaugurated the phase of modernity, was based on the centrality of 'wage labour', and its accompaniments in the commodity-factory mode of production, post-modern society, as Bauman writes, is generated by 'consumer conduct', which implies "consumer freedom geared to the consumer market". Individuals are engaged (morally by society, functionally by social system) first and foremost as consumers than producers. Consumer freedom, which was a mere 'squatter' in the era of modernity, moves over to a central position of 'legitimate resident'. The substitution of consumer freedom as the hub around which the life-world rotates, now changes the Freudian assumption of the antagonistic relationship between the 'pleasure principle' and the 'reality principle'. For the consumer, the reality is not the enemy of pleasure.

These processes also bring about rapid changes in the notions of state, nation, democracy and territory. Economic and cultural globalization, emergence of global diaspora, expansion of market, financial capital and banking, revolution in the technology of communication through telephony, internet, fax, e-mail, etc., are increasingly abridging the power of the state. These have also rendered the classical ideas about nation-state and territory highly elastic and subject to external and internal factors often beyond its control. The imperatives of high technology uses in affairs of public administration, and in strategic planning and expansion of matters related to economy, defence and international relations, radically alter the autonomy and power of political leadership, and change the context of political responsibility. This partly explains the recent debates in political science and public administration about the 're-invention of democracy' and 'the state'. These substantive changes in the social structure and values of society in the post-modern phase have a very close linkage with the beginning of the cultural and philosophical debate in sociology.

Obviously, during the past few decades, sociology has been attempting to come to terms with post-modernity. Its substantial representation is where post-modernity is treated as a symptom of a crisis brought about by the post-industrial economic, cultural and technological challenges. This has contributed to creative innovations in methods and concepts, or even in the theoretic paradigms of sociology, such as we witness in the cases of phenomenological, ethnomethodological and dramaturgical sociologies. Attempt is made to render sociology more relevant to comprehend the post-modern social and cultural conditions. In this process, sociology has faced challenges, which have led it to be subsumed in the cultural hubris of post-modernity, particularly, in its epistemological and ontological assumptions, whose instances we may find in extreme applications of Garfinkel's ethnomethodology or in Goffman's dramaturgy, both of which question the authenticity of meanings in sociological discourse. But, in these instances too, the extent to which their paradigms imply the necessity to decode meanings or demystification of sociological stances, they continue to accept the validity of social reality as an ontological presence and as an objective reality.

The focus on sociology of post-modernity is, otherwise, pre-eminent in the works of other mainstream sociologists, such as Pierre Bourdieu, Anthony Giddens and Alain Touraine. Bourdieu may not have anchored sociology primarily in the notion of a social system or social order; he prefers to use the concept of a 'field' but field is a social-cultural arena where agents enter into relationships and form strategies as per their 'habitus' to augment access to social, economic and cultural capital, to position themselves in society. Although, the role of the individual is denied, the concept of habitus still links Bourdieu's sociology to culture-society-personality matrix, which is central to a theory of social order and social change in the classical sociology. Similarly, Touraine's emphasis on social movement and social action gives centrality to the place of 'rational-subject' in the processes of configuration of society, thus, it rescues sociology denying its 'rejection' implicit in most post-modernist philosophy. Touraine writes: "There can be no modernization without rationalization, but that modernity also means the formation of the subject in the world who can take responsibility for themselves and for society". Giddens too reiterates the significance of the subject and the formation of 'self-identity' in the post-modern society in order to establish protective relationships to safeguard against the uncertainties of this society. Society constitutes a social order in a process of change whose direction of which remains uncertain and the identity of individual problematic. He defines structure as a process which constitutes itself through motivated agents and their interaction, and exists through, what he terms as 'structuration'. The concept of structuration, according to him, adds dynamism in social analysis of systems that are increasingly flexible, open to influence of plurality and have loosely coordinated power centres. Evidently, the sociology of post-modernity continues to make strategic conceptual and methodological responses to the challenges of post modernity.

It is, therefore, essential that sociology as it encounters post-modernity remains consistent in its commitment to studying order and change by adopting strategies of innovative exegesis and extension in its conceptual and methodological repertoire. The imperative of studying post-modernity itself as a product of the post-industrial phase of global capitalism should continue to engage sociologists. Among the classical sociologists, Marx more than Max Weber or Durkheim, was able to anticipate the cultural and structural logic of transformation of the industrial capitalism to its next phase of post-industrial evolution—a phase in which the inner contradictions of the processes of rationalization would yield to forces of perpetual impermanence and estrangement of human consciousness. The social and cultural attributes of the post-modern society confirm this in large measure. We may thus conclude: "Proper analysis of post-modern condition brings us, therefore, back into the orthodox area of sociological investigation (though an area now structured in an orthodox way). This means that rather than seeking a new form of a post-modern sociology (a sociology attuned to its style, as an 'intellectual genre', to the cultural climate of post-modernity) sociologists should be engaged in developing a sociology of post-modernity (i.e., deploying the strategy of systemic, rational discourse to the task of constructing a theoretical model of post-modern society as a system in its own right, rather than a distorted form, or an aberration from another system" (see, Bauman, 1989: 61).

It seems to me to have a great relevance for Indian sociologists who are observing a slow but inevitable process of movement towards modernization or even post-modernization of society. Here, the persistence of the cultural and structural features of multiple and mixed historicities constitutes a very relevant framework for comparative analysis at the substantive level of social realities. It should also be interesting to evaluate as to how the Indian sociology and social sciences have perceived and encountered the challenges of modernity and incipient post-modernity.

Notes

1. Reinhart Bendix, *Nation-building and Citizenship*, New York: John Wiley and Sons, Inc., 1964.

S.N. Eisenstadt, "Social Transformation in Modernization", American Sociological Review, 30, No. 5, October, 1965, pp. 659-73.

Lucian Pye, *Politics, Personality and Nation-building: Burma's Search for Identity*, New Haven: Yale University Press, 1963.

Daniel Lerner, *The Passing of Traditional Society: Modernizing the Middle-East*, New York: The Free Press, 1966.

Robert N. Kearney, *Politics and Modernization in South and South East Asia*, New York: John Wiley and Sons, 1975.

Harvey G. Kebschull, *Politics in Transitional Societies*, New York: Appleton-Century-Crofts, 1968.

Reuven Kahane, *The Problem of Political Legitimacy in an Antagonistic Society: The Indonesia Case*, Beverly Hill: Sage Publications, 1973.

2. W.E. Moore, *Social Change*, p. 88.
3. K.N. Jha, *Women Towards Modernization*, Janki Prakashan, Patna, 1985, p. 13.
4. S.S. Mathur, *A Sociological Approach to Indian Education*, 1997, pp. 74-75.
5. Yogendra Singh, *Essays on Modernization in India*, Manohar, New Delhi, 1978, pp. 1-2.
6. Ibid., p. 2.
7. Ibid., pp. 3-4.
8. Ibid., pp. 7-8.
9. Ibid., p. 8.
10. Ibid., pp. 9-10.
11. Ibid., pp. 10-11.
12. Yogendra Singh, *Modernization of Indian Tradition*, Rawat Publications, Jaipur, 1988 (Reprint), p. 205.
13. Karl W. Deutsch, "Social Mobilization and Political Development", *The American Political Science Review*, Vol. LV, No. 3, September 1961.
14. Daniel Lerner and Wibur Schramm, *Communication and Change in the Developing Countries*, (ed.), Honolulu East Center Press, 1967.
15. In this connection see:

    David Apter, *Politics of Modernization*, Chicago: University of Chicago Press, 1965.

    Lucian Pye and Sidney Verba, *Political Culture and Political Development*, Princeton: Princeton University Press, 1965.

Geertz Clifford, *Old Societies and New States: The Quest for Modernity in Asia and Africa*, New York: Free Press of Glencoe, 1963.

G.A. Almond and Sidney Verba, *The Civic Culture*, Boston and Toronto: Little Brown and Co., 1965.

16. See:

Edward C. Banfield, *The Moral of a Backward Society*, Glencoe Illinois: The Free Press, 1958.

David C. McClelland, *The Achieving Society*, New York: Van Nostrand, 1961.

Everett E. Hagen, *On The Theory of Social Change*, Honewood, Illinois: The Dorset Press, Inc., 1962.

R.N. Bellah, *Religion and Progress in Modern Asia*, American Sociological Review, 1964.

17. M.J. Levy, *Modernization and the Structure of Societies*, Vol. I and II, Princeton: Princeton University Press, 1966.

(Also see the approach of the economists who identify modernization with capacity for capital mobilization and investment in industries, for example, W.W. Rostow, *The Stages of Economic Growth: A Non-Communist Manifesto*, Cambridge University Press. 1960)

18. (The importance of 'initial condition' of social structure, culture and resources has been emphasized by several social scientists: this determines the prospect and pattern of modernization.)

Jr. M.J. Levy, *Contrasting Factors in the Modernization of China and Japan, Economic Growth: Brazil, India, Japan* (ed.), Simon Kuznets, Wilbert. E. Moore and Joseph J. Spegler, Durhun, N.C.: Duke University Press, 1955, pp. 496-97.

S.N. Eisenstadt, "Transformation of Social, Political and Cultural Orders in Modernization", American Sociological Review, Vol. 30, No. 5, October 1965.

G. Myrdal, Asian Drama (chap. 14).

19. S.N. Eisenstadt, op. cit. (Supra).
20. Yogendra Singh, op. cit., p. 205.
21. (Structural-functional approach is one of the commonest ones in the studies on modernization. Works of Parsons, Eisenstadt, Apter, Shils, Jr. Marion J. Levy, etc. as cited above are good illustrations).
22. W.F. Wertheim, *East-West Parallels*, The Hague: W. Van Hague Ltd., 1968.

Irving L. Horowitz, Three Worlds of Development, New York: Oxford University Press, 1966.

23. Talcott Parsons, "Evolutionary Universals in Society", *American Sociological Review*, Vol. 29, No. 3, June 1964.
24. Bendix Gusfield and Yogendra Singh, op. cit.
25. I.L. Horowitz and G. Myrdal.
26. A.A. Zovorikine, "Some Problems of the Theory of Culture", *Socialist Digest*, No. 2, June, 1968, pp. 68 and 96.
27. Gary L. Buck and Alvin L. Jacobson, "Some Problems of the Structural-Functional Analysis: An Empirical Test", *American Sociological Review*, Vol. 33, No. 3, June, pp. 343-55.
28. Buck and Jacobson, op. cit.
29. Yogendra Singh, op. cit., p. 206.
30. G. Myrdal, op. cit.
31. Yogendra Singh, op. cit., p. 207.
    (also see, Buck and Jacobson, op. cit.)
32. See:
    Irving L. Horowitz, op. cit.
    John B. Stephenson, "Is Everyone Going Modern? A Critique and a Suggestion for Measuring Modernism", *The American Journal of Sociology*, 74, No. 3, November 1968, pp. 265-67.
    J.P. Nettle and Ronald Robertson, *International Systems and Modernization of Societies*, New York: Basic Books, Inc., 1968.
    C.E. Black, *The Dynamics of Modernization*, New York: Harper and Row, 1967.
    Daniel Lerner, op. cit.
33. David Apter, *The Political Kingdom of Wganda*, New Jersey: Princeton University Press, 1961, p. 22.
34. Ibid., p. 24.
35. Ibid., pp. 25-27.
36. Robert T. Holt and John E. Turner, *The Political Basis of Economic Development: An Exploration in Comparative Political Analysis*, D. Van Nostrand Co., New Jersey, 1966, p. 7.
37. Thedosius Dobzhansky, *Mankind Evolving: The Evolution of the Human Species*, New Haven: Yale University Press, 1963, pp. 337-38.
38. Lucian Pye, op. cit., p. 44.
39. Ibid., p. 44.
40. David McClelland, op. cit., pp. 46-57.

41. Alfred Diament, *Political Development: Approach to Development: Politics, Administration and Change*, (ed.), John D. Montgomery and William J. Siffins, New York: Mc Graw Hill Book Co., 1966, p. 44.
42. Edward Shils, *The Intellectual Between Tradition and Modernity: The Indian Situation*, The Hague: Mouton, 1961.
43. D.K. Vajpeyi, *Modernization and Social change in India*, Manohar, New Delhi, 1979, p. 6.
44. Ibid., pp. 6-7.
45. (A) S.C. Dube, *Human Problems of Economic Development in Economic Development and Cultural Change*, Ithaca: Cornell University Press, 1965.

    (B) S.C. Dube, "Modernization and its Adaptive Demands on Indian Society, papers on the Sociology of Education in India", (eds.), M.S. Gore, I.P. Desai and Suma Chitnis, National Council of Educational Research and Training, New Delhi, 1967.
46. Ibid., p. 37.
47. Ibid., p. 35.
48. D.K. Vajpeyi, op. cit., p. 8.
49. Ibid.
50. S.C. Dube, Human, op. cit., p. 38.
51. Ibid., pp. 40-45.
52. D.K. Vajpeyi, op. cit., p. 9.
53. Yogendra Singh, op. cit., p. 121.
54. D.K. Vajpeyi, op. cit., pp. 54-55.
55. W.W. Rostow, *Stages of Economic Growth*, New York: Cambridge University Press, 1960.
56. R.N. Bellah, "Religious Revolution", *American Sociological Review*, 29, No. 3, June, 1964, pp. 358-74.
57. D.K. Vajpeyi, op. cit., p. 12.
58. A.J. Toynbee, *A Study of History*, Vol. 8, London: Oxford University Press, 1963.
59. D.K. Vajpeyi, op. cit., p. 13.
60. Yogendra Singh, op. cit., pp. 202-4.
61. Ibid., pp. 208-13.
62. Ibid., pp. 213-15.
63. Yogendra Singh, *Ideology and Theory in Indian Sociology*, Rawat Publications, Jaipur and New Delhi, 2004, pp. 33-38.

References

Baudrillard, Jean, *Simulacres et Simulation*, Paris: Galilee, 1981.

Bauman, Zygmunt, "Sociological Response to Post-modernity", Thesis Eleven, 1989.

Bourdieu, Pierre and Wacquant, L.J.D., *An Invitation to Reflexive Sociology*, Chicago: University of Chicago Press, 1992.

Clifford, Geertz, *Social Change and Economic Modernization in Two Indonesian Towns: A Case in Point, on the Theory of Social Change*, (ed.) Everett E. Hagen, Illinois: The Dorsey Press, Inc., 1962.

Cohn, Bernard S., *Notes on the History of the Study of Indian Society and Culture, Structure and Change in Indian Sociology*, (ed.), Singer and Cohn, Chicago: Aldine Publishing Company, 1968.

Derrida, Jacques, *The Margins of Philosophy*, Sussex: Harvester Press, 1982.

Deutsch, Karl W., "Social Mobilization and Political Development", The *American Political Science Review*, Vol. LV, No. 3 (September), 1961.

Giddens, Anthony, *Consequences of Modernity*, Cambridge: Polity, 1990.

—, *Modernity and Self-Identity: Self and Society in a Late Modern Age*, Cambridge: Polity, 1992.

Gusfield, Joseph R., "Tradition and Modernity: Misplaced Polarities in the Study of Social Change", *American Journal of Sociology*, Vol. 72, No. 4 (January), 1967.

Jameson, Fredric, *Post-modernism and Consumer Society, in Post-modernism and its Discontents: Theories and Practices*, by E.A. Kaplan (ed.), New York: Verso, 1988.

Jha, Kali Nath and Vinita Singh, "Sexuality and the Markets: A Study of Women Migrant Workers in Ranchi", paper presented in the XXIX All India Sociological Conference, Udaipur, December 21-23, 2003.

—, "Women 'Haria' Sellers: At Cross Roads", paper presented in the National Seminar on 'Tribes, State Policies and NGOs organized by the Indian Anthropological Association, New Delhi, March 26-27, 2004.

Lerner, Daniel and Wilbur Schramm, (ed.) *Communication and Change in the Developing Countries*, Honolulu East West Center Press, 1967.

Rudolph, Lloyd I., "The Modernity of Tradition: The Democratic Incarnation of Caste in India", *American Political Science Review*, Vol. LIX, No. 4 (December), 1965.

Sharma, K.L., *Reconceptualising Caste, Class and Tribe*, Rawat Publications, Jaipur and New Delhi, 2001.

Singh, Yogendra, *Indian Sociology: Social Conditioning and Emerging Concerns*, Vistaar Publications, New Delhi, 1986.

—, "The Desired Role of Political Leadership in Economic Reforms", in *Indian Economy and the Institutional Set-up*, in J.L. Bajaj (ed.) Delhi: Policy Group, 1999.

—, *Culture Change in India: Identity and Globalization*, Rawat Publications, Jaipur and New Delhi, 2000.

Touraine, Alain, *Critique of Modernity*, Oxford: Blackwell, 1995.

3

Modernization and Women's Studies

The sociologists of the present age have paid attention to the scientific analysis of the modernization process. Along with theoretical discussion, efforts have been made to analyse the modernization process in different parts of the world. A number of sociological studies have been conducted for analysing the modernization process in the area of women's studies in relation to different societies.

One important study of modernization was conducted by Daniel Lerner, in the countries of Middle East. Lerner has conducted the study in Iran, Turkey and Lebanon, and made a comparative analysis of modernization taking place in those countries. Lerner also analysed the relevance of different factors in the modernization process. He discussed the cases of different or varying degrees of modernization in different countries. Daniel Lerner has presented the study through his book, *The Passing of Traditional Society*. In this book, he first examines the concept of modernization and the relationship between modernization and westernization in these countries. He points out: "The ethnocentric predicament is confounded by the failure to realise that modernization appears as westernization by historical coincidence. Modernity is primarily a state of mind, acceptance of progress, propensity to growth, readiness to adapt oneself to change. The relation of the North Atlantic area first developed the social processes—secularization, urbanization, industrialization, popular participation by which this state of mind came to prevail. The 'western model' is only historically western; sociologically it is global. The recent history of USSR and Japan shows how effectively these processes can modernize societies that are geographically remote from the west."[1] The data in this book shows that the same basic model reappears in virtually all modernizing societies in all the continents regardless of variations in race, colour or creed.

The western model of modernization is not confined to western societies; rather it has appeared in all modernizing societies and hence it may be called a global model. It is western only in the sense that it first appeared in the western countries due to the technological achievements, scientific inventions, industrialization and urbanization. Hence, it is a historical coincidence that modernization became a western model because of its first appearance in the west.

Dealing with the concept of east-west modernization that is the east under the impact of west, Daniel Lerner has pointed out "From the west came the stimuli which undermined traditional society in the middle east; for reconstruction of a modern society that will operate efficiently in the world today the west is still a useful model. What the west is, in this sense, the Middle East seeks to become. But these societies in a hurry had little patience with the historical process of western development; what happened in the west over centuries, some Easterns now seek to accomplish in years."[2]

He further observes: "Moreover they thought to do it their own way. A complication of Middle East modernization is its own ethnocentrism expressed politically in extreme nationalism, psychologically in passionate zenophobia. The hatred shown by anti colonialism is harvested in the rejection of every appearance of foreign tutelage. Wanted are modern institutions but not modern ideologies, modern power but not modern purposes, modern wealth but not wisdom, modern commodities but not modern cant. It is not clear however, that modest ways and words can be shown easily and so totally sundered.

Underlying the varying ideological forms which modernization took in Europe, America, Russia, (and Japan), there have been certain behavioural institutional compulsions common to all."[3]

Modernization in the countries of Middle East has been under the influence of westernization but the process of modernization in these countries has been different from that in the western countries. Modernization started much earlier in the western world and the modern state of modernization appeared after a long period. But the people of the Middle East countries want to get modernized without any loss of time and do not show any patience for the transition of a traditional society into a modern society. This process of transformation of a traditional into a modern society does not involve only accepting and adopting material comforts and technological achievements. It also involves a change in operation, outlook, approach, manners and patterns of behaviour. These changes in the inner aspects of social life and personality structure cannot take place at one stroke and in a limited short time. The people of Middle Eastern countries, are in a hurry to become modern and have not been in a position to internalise modern norms and values. They want to enjoy the material comforts of the west but without developing the wisdom and knowledge necessary for achieving these material comforts. In other words, they become modernized through imitating the explicit aspects of modern society without adopting and internalising the implicit aspects.

Daniel Lerner has come to the conclusion that modernization has a positive relation with urbanization, education, democratization and media of mass communication. In his own words, 'High multiple correlations were found between urbanization, literacy, media participation and politics participation, each correlated in turn with the other three'.[4] It means that if modernization increases, there is development in all these four variables. In the same way, if any of these four variables changes, there is a change in the state in modernity. Moreover, the positive correlation suggests that with the spread of mass education, or the development of mass participation or mass communication or with the growth of urbanization, modernization advances. Lerner has specifically examined the role of education in democratization and modernization of a society among the three countries of Turkey, Lebanon and Iran. He concludes that Turkey is more modernized and Iran, is the least modernized among the three countries. He also pointed out that among the countries of Latin America, percentage of literacy is lower than that in Iran and hence these countries are more backward and traditional than Iranian society. This study suggests that the degree of urbanism, literacy, mass participation and mass communication are the indices of modernity.

Another important study was conducted by Philip in Ghana. He studied the Ghanaians who received western education in Ghana or who were educated in the west. Foster analysed the role of education in the modernization of the people. Foster came to the conclusion that western education created a climate favourable to development and innovations. Referring to this study, Mathur made his observation as under: "Foster came to the conclusion that it was formal western schooling in Ghana that created a cultural environment in which innovation could take place. He also found that those were the most cultured Ghanaians, the western educated elites-who not only achieved independence but also developed the political—cultural ideas to go with it."[5] It means that western education developed a modern outlook in them and they developed innovational ideas which resulted in the achievement of independence and changes in the political system.

Edward Shils conducted a study in 1961, in India, to analyse the role of intellectuals in bridging the gap between traditional and modern societies. This study has come out in his book *The Intellectuals between Tradition and Modernity: The Indian Situation*. Shils comes to the conclusion: "If there is to be only successful bridging of the gap between traditional and modern societies, it is the western educated intellectual who must perform the task."[6] It is evident from this remark that the factor of education plays a vital role in changing a traditional society and bringing it, closer to a modern society. It is obvious that such a change may be possible only through the process of modernization. Hence, it may be stated that Shils' study highlights the role of education in the process of modernization.

The eminent Indian sociologist, Yogendra Singh conducted a study on university teachers in Rajasthan at Jaipur. The purpose of the study was to find out the extent of modernity among the university teachers. As regards the method used by Yogendra Singh in conducting this study, he has himself remarked: "The study has been conducted among teachers at the University of Rajasthan in the faculties of arts, science, commerce and law at Jaipur. In other faculties the university does not teach directly: Instruction is given in affiliated colleges (run by the state government or private management). We confined our study to the teachers of the university departments because of many structural aspects—mode of recruitment, service conditions, facilities and emoluments as well as the academic environment—the teachers in affiliated colleges have basic differences compared to those in the university teaching departments. We assume that these differences in existential conditions do influence the values, attitudes and role structures of the teachers in relation to modernization."[7]

In the present study, only the teachers of university departments were covered. In 1969-70, there were in all 460 teachers—of which 356 were male teachers. Among them 21 were Professors, 68 Readers, 8 Senior Lecturers and 259 Lecturers. A sample was not drawn and a total universe of 356 male teachers was studied. A structured questionnaire was prepared to conduct the fieldwork and each teacher was supplied one structured questionnaire. Out of 356 questionnaires supplied, only 248 were returned and the analysis was made on the basis of information contained in those returned questionnaires. The respondents were divided into two categories, junior and senior. The senior lecturers, readers and professors were placed in the senior categories. The items contained in the questionnaire were concerned with enquiries about aspiration, commitment, morale and authoritarianism. Referring to the objective of the study, Yogendra Singh pointed out: "The emphasis is on measurement of the levels of modernization, aspiration, commitment, morale, and authoritarianism among the teachers. For our measures we sought reliability, but this pilot enquiry offers no definitive statement about the role-structure of teachers in relation to modernization. The analysis does, however, achieve a precise insight into the nature of role-structures and the integration of values in relation to modernization among university teachers. It is hoped that these findings would:

(1) offer specific insights into the process of modernization in the macro-structures, and
(2) contribute to the sociology of the profession and their culture, relevant to the theme of modernization in India."[8]

Yogendra Singh has drawn certain conclusions:

(1) In his own words, "evidently, recruitment into the teaching profession entails inter-generational mobility within the set of occupations characterized as the professions: this is mobility within an occupational stratum and not between strata; and its pattern reflects the dominance of urban groups and professional classes".[9]
(2) He has also come to the conclusion that "the teachers are significantly more educated than their fathers. 29 percent teachers' fathers were barely literate, and only 33.1 percent had university education; 25.8 percent of the teachers' fathers were educated up to high school and intermediate standard. Evidently,. inter-generational mobility in respect of education has been high for those who teach at the

university, suggesting a diversification of educational opportunities".[10]

(3) The teachers have their own cognition of modernity. The responses were grouped into four categories:
(a) universalistic structural,
(b) universalistic ideology,
(c) psychic and cultural mobility, and
(d) superficial symbolism.

The first, universalistic structural, includes such reported traits as industrialization, technological growth, etc. The second, universalistic ideology, includes responses like rationalism, scientific attitude, pragmatism, etc. The category, psychic and cultural mobility, includes characteristics emphasising tolerance, equality, egalitarianism, and other related attributes. All these three categories connote a positive cognition of modernity. The fourth category, superficial symbolism, includes those reported characteristics which had a negative connotation and had to do with style of life, such as fashionableness, superficiality in dress, ostentation, new mannerisms, etc. Those who perceive modernity thus also disapprove of it.[11]

(4) Analysing the findings further, Yogendra Singh has come to the following conclusions: "Modernization connotes to most teachers not technological attributes but rather an universalistic ideology: social reform measures, better inter-group understanding and psychic mobility, suggesting that they view modernity as a system of operative norms rather than of fundamental values. The emphasis is on contingency and relativity more than on absolute qualities. Factor analysis of items in the modernization scale yields two important dimensions for the teachers: *affective-neutrality* and *universalism*. This suggests that the major psycho-cultural contingency in the evaluation of modernity tends to be that of kinship and values. In societies where kinship bonds and loyalties have been salient traditionally, these impinge deeply upon a

role-structure in the process of modernization, and value-supports are needed to transform these rational principles into modern forms. The conflict in the teachers' modernization process, therefore, tends to be between primordial and universal principles role-definitions."[12]

Apart from the above study, Yogendra Singh has contributed a number of books, articles, speeches and trained younger generations of sociologists for the study of societies in India. We have no words to assess the contributions of Yogendra Singh but without doubt, Singh has established a new trend in sociological literature.

Most of the studies on urban population are on students, adolescents, and middle class families, mainly confined to their opinion and attitude, interests and personality patterns. Kapur,[13] Merchant,[14] Cormack,[15] Shah,[16] Jha,[17] Mathew,[18] Hallen,[19] and Mitra,[20] are among them.

K.T. Merchant's investigation among educated urban college girls and boys and middle-aged persons was conducted by the questionnaire method. A few of the findings suggest that even at that time the 'personal conception of marriage' was gaining ground against the ideal that marriage was a sacrament, and a majority (nearly 78%) of the urban-educated girls favoured marriage by choice. A sense of social responsibility was gaining ground among them, and their attitudes had considerably changed, especially towards their own status, modernity as well as marriage and the family.

In spite of its methodological limitations (response was only 4.9%), Merchant's work is distinctly a pioneering study. It is of great value since it raises many issues for further research.

Margaret L. Cormack's study, though on a fairly common issue, viz., the state of higher education in India, is somewhat unusual. It aims to evaluate the Indian college and university students' awareness of and attitude towards social change and modernization in India.

The study presents the psycho-cultural analysis of the puzzling phenomena of 'corruption', 'party-politics' and 'indiscipline' among the college and university students in India. The most encouraging and significant overall conclusion of the study is that India's real problem is not 'student indiscipline', 'corruption' or 'party-politics' but the deeper phenomenon of social change, which is significantly influenced by culture, and it is consciously moulded by democracy and education. If properly moulded, the culture could divert the organised student discontent into social dynamism. Thus, it advocates the case for higher and proper education suitable to the changed socio-cultural context of India. The study ends with a message of hope that with improved conditions of teaching and learning, Indian universities would be able to prepare their students to meet the challenges of tomorrow.

Cormack also focuses on the changing attitudes of female university and college students towards education, marriage, types of marriage, types of mate that they would prefer to have, husband-wife relationship and women's place in India, and so on. Her findings point towards their attitudes changing and becoming modern. Yet the change is very limited. Even with its limitations of not having scientific sampling of the institutes and of having voluntary respondents which the author herself has mentioned, which does not enable her to generalize about any one particular group. The study undoubtedly generates several theoretical formulations and leads which need to be validated through much needed thorough and scientific research in this very important area.

Cormack's study is a portrayal of women of India and examines the persistence of tradition and change. The informants were undergraduate women students of Columbia University, coming from educated, urban, middle, and upper class backgrounds, representing various geographical areas. Most of the women were Hindu, but the group included a Muslim, a Sikh, and a Christian. Those informants were interviewed and they responded to a set of questions, most of which were open-ended. Supplemented by the author's own observations and experiences of a long stay in India during her childhood and early adulthood, the study sought to discover how Indian girls internalized the traditional feminine role. It was found that Hindu women by and large are tradition oriented and accept social customs and values that are widely accepted by the society. Traditions of Hinduism in India are very old and deep, and since no culture breaks entirely with the past, tradition continues to play a vigorous role in culture change. Hindu women while responding to society's changing needs continue selectively to adhere to their traditional roles and value system.

The most serious limitation of the study is that it is based primarily on information supplied by only ten undergraduate women students who did not represent a cross-section of Indian women. And this information could be inadequate, insufficient, biased or even unreliable. However, this limitation was overcome by the author's unusual insight and the wealth of knowledge she had which resulted in an exceptional work.[21]

The situation after the partition of the country was such that economic oppression almost compelled women of even orthodox middle class families to take up a variety of jobs which were previously not considered respectable for women. The number of educated working women engaged in various occupations has since been increasing. Working in offices as clerks, private secretaries, telephone operators, receptionists, officers, in the foreign and administrative services, commercial centres and similar other places has become common. Social, political and economic change in the country have drawn the attention of scholars and social scientists towards the changed situation and the emerging class of urban women.[22]

Rama Mehta's study[23] deals with a segment of urban women. This study was undertaken with a view to examining the complex and far-reaching impact of western education and influence on Indian society. The study seeks to find out to what extent traditional customs and values are still operative in society and in what ways and how far the long western domination over India has changed the attitudes of the elite of the country.

This study starts with the assumption that Hindu tradition are bound up with domestic rituals and customs held and perpetuated mainly by women, and that the impact of alien influences on them greatly undermine their faith in traditional norms and values. It also assumes that though the foreign political domination has not been able to alter the traditional pattern of society because of the overwhelming majority living in rural India, it has effectively changed the attitudes of the elite of the country. So with these two assumptions the study chose to examine the attitudes of a sample of fifty western-educated Hindu women. The sample comprised Hindu women from different castes and provinces in India, having a minimum educational qualification of a B.A. degree from an Indian university, and having received school education in a Christian school, where English was the medium of instruction. These women were chosen out of the age-group twenty to twenty-five in 1947 and were all married and had parents who were either in the army or civil service.

The study seeks to assess the influence of western education on this group and to find out whether its impact resulted in merely a superficial imitation of western ways of living or it went deeper and affected their values, findings, and ways of thinking. The study also analyses the impact of two different value systems—western and traditional Hindu—and two different ways of living, operating simultaneously on the respondents. Because the family background of the parents of most of the respondents was tradition centred, the study also attempts to examine what traditional values were retained and passed on to the younger generation.

The attitudes of western—educated Hindu women towards education, Hinduism, caste marriage, male-female relationships, dowry, divorce, upbringing of children, their education and recreation, and child-parent relationship, have been studied. While enquiring about their views on these issues, their own backgrounds and conditions in their parental homes were also recorded. This was done with a view to examining the kinds of influence that moulded their attitudes and how effective the influence was in determining the respondents' views in later life.

The tools utilised for data collection were on open-ended questionnaire personally handed over to the subjects, followed by in-depth interviews conducted by the author who is herself a sociologist by training. For purposes of analysis, the views expressed at the time of the interviews were taken to represent their attitudes.

The study points towards a limited change in the basic attitudes of western-educated Hindu women towards traditionalism versus modernity. The analysis of their responses do amply indicate change by way of their no longer being committed to the traditional institutions, but it also shows that they do continue to be intellectually committed to the traditional value system. The study indicates that western education, and their stay abroad had resulted in lessening their faith in traditional institutions, such as caste and Hindu religious obligations, and in their superficially imitating the west with regard to the patterns of living and behaving, and that of their leisure time as well as work activities and interests, but it had not gone deeper into them, and had not changed the traditional value system and had not led to the assimilation of the western ways of thinking and feeling. The Hindu traditional values and attitudes in the domestic realm were, by and large, very much approved and the western attitudes were condemned, particularly towards marriage and family obligations, parent-child relationship, male-female relationship, and sex-freedom. But all this persistence of tradition and emergence of limited change was due to the fact that most of the respondents' parents' home backgrounds and ways of life were traditional, from which they had assimilated their values.

In the process of modernization, they do favour change, but on the foundation of their cultural values. They do approve of taking full advantage of modern opportunities but without becoming western in their outlook and without adopting western ideals. They felt a great need of synthesizing the old or the traditional with the new or modern and that a balance between the two should be maintained. The analysis of the data also asserts that maintaining traditional values without the traditional way of life was almost impossible. That is why it was doubtful whether the traditional value system, though fundamentally sound, could survive in the face of modernization.

Limitations of the study lie in the fact that it is silent about the way in which the author went about selecting the sample units, and how and in what situation they were interviewed. The questionnaire or the interview guide is also not described explicitly anywhere. The sample is very limited as well as not truly representative of its group.[24]

Yet, as a pioneering effort in studying western-educated Hindu urban women, it is commendable. One of the significant contributions of the study is in the area of methodology of data collection. The study has demonstrated through experimentation and empirical investigation that a questionnaire alone without a follow-up interview in depth is inadequate in an inquiry which aims to study the attitudes and reactions towards significant issues beyond the superficial level.[25]

'The Educated Women in Indian Society',[26] a study carried out by the YWCA of India in 1971, is an honest and fruitful attempt to draw attention towards the educated women in India who, though they comprise a small section of our society, are qualitatively very significant for the nation.[27]

Rhoda L. Goldstein's study[28] is empirical and has a sociological perspective. It attempts to investigate empirically urban middle class women who had recently graduated from universities in India. It focuses on the ways in which a group of young highly educated urban middle class women (and their families) deal with their expanded status. It is a probing research into some important issues, such as how the roles engendered by university education are made to mesh with the traditional, family-centred female roles how these educated women perceive the effect of higher education on their lives and their perception of female roles; and what are the problems that they face when they take up jobs. Critical analysis explores how the forces of tradition and modernity are working and how problems stemming from these are resolved. How and to what extent women having university education and consequent employment alter their roles and create new values and norms, constitutes the running theme of the entire book.

For studying social change, a sample of 97 young women graduates and postgraduates were selected from the women who graduated from Bangalore University in 1965. The research revealed that the majority of educated women (63%) feel that education helps in finding a suitable match. The bachelor's degree is becoming acceptable and functional for urban middle class women, but higher education—more than a bachelor's degree—is still not considered likely to enhance a woman's marriage marketability. A large majority (85%) of these women believed that education helps in adjusting in marriage.

Another interesting finding is the answer to the question as to how by virtue of their education, they were expected to contribute to society: while only four percent answered the contribution through one's own household, family or children, the majority of the answers reflected their expectations to use their education in vocational fields. The notion that educated women can contribute through paid position is relatively new and suggests the development of new interests outside the home.

The study suggests that both opportunities for and people's attitudes towards middle class women's employment have changed. In Bangalore work has become an established pattern rather than an exception for educated women. The study suggests that higher education enables women to become aware of the alternatives to marriage and work as a career, which is now becoming a reality for urban middle class women.

The researcher rightly feels that the pattern found by Levy in modern China, in which educated women preferred spinsterhood to unsuitable marriages may well get repeated in India. However, the majority of graduates and postgraduate women under study rarely consider acting against the expressed wishes of their parents or husbands in matters of 'taking up jobs'. None of the women were found questioning women's dependence on male relatives as chaperones throughout their life, even while many of them maintain that a woman can be happy without marriage provided she is employed. They continue to recognise the married state and motherhood as the prime goals through which women gain recognition, though their desire to work is stimulated by their wish to be 'independent' and to have some individual income to meet their personal needs.

Education and employment are beginning to be viewed as tools which lead to greater independence and more equality for women. At the same time, the new freedom and opportunities are still combined with old restrictions and traditional notions about women's dependence on male protection. Thus, the study reports co-existence of the new and old and predicts a gradual change.

There are some methodological inconsistencies in Goldstein's study. The method of investigation is not similar for all the sample units: in the majority of cases the questionnaires were personally administered in an interview situation, whereas to a majority of respondents, questionnaires were administered by mail. The information could have been hopefully more reliable if it had been collected through a uniform method. The situation of investigation is also not consistent for all the respondents: while 44 percent of women were interviewed in privacy, in the presence of one or more family members, a majority of the respondents were interviewed in the company of their friends. A consistent interview situation of a single investigator interviewing each respondent individually would have elicited more consistent and reliable information without colouring the views by the presence of relatives or friends. Then, the sample selected for the study is too small, especially considering the fact that she had three research assistants to help her. A large sample, possibly selected out of four universities—one from each of the four geographical zones of India—would have greatly enhanced the value of the book. In any case, Bangalore does not adequately represent India which is full of cultural diversities and regional representations.[29]

The study by Promilla Kapur[30] in 1973 is one of the systematic large-scale empirical studies which aim at assessing the changes in the attitudes of young urban middle class educated working women in India towards three vital aspects of life—love, marriage and sex. In this study, Kapur comes to the conclusion that India has experienced significant changes in various aspects of life in the last seven decades or so. Various facets of its society are in the process of transition from a traditional to a modern way of life. The pace of socio-economic and political change has been greatly accelerated after independence, when the constitution recognised and proclaimed the equality of man and woman in all domains of life. The various acts and statutes imparted to women various privileges and rights, along with the increasing opportunities for education and employment.[31]

S.K. Kuthiala's study appears in the book, *From Tradition to Modernity*.[32] It examines the social effects of industry on a representative sample of villagers who were pushed into the industrial labour force from their rural base. These samples were drawn from two industrial towns—one in Punjab and the other in Haryana—obtaining their labour force from the surrounding rural areas. Kuthiala's work analyses only one aspect of the movement of Indian villages from tradition to modernity—the participation of a section of the village people in urban industry. But this is an important aspect and it needed to be investigated carefully. In his own words, "My effort in this research work is to focus on a particular aspect of modernization in India, and that is of industrial employment of rural labour force. We selected industrial workers maintaining traditional rural residential locations to assess what social and economic factors are causing the rural labour force to join industrial occupations, what effects the occupational experiences have in reshaping traditional and modern values, and future orientation. It is apparent in this study that individuals are not always ready to relinquish their traditional forms of knowledge for a journey into the uncertainty of the future."[33]

The study by D.K. Vajpeyi came out in the book, *Modernization and Social Change in India*[34] in 1979. The study focuses on changes which have occurred due to political participation, mass media exposure and empathy in the attitudes of citizens of a north Indian state—Uttar Pradesh—over a ten-year period, 1966-1976. The first phase of the study was conducted in 1966, the second in 1972, and the final phase was completed in 1976.

Vajpeyi has come to the conclusion that 'In our findings, media exposure, urbanism and cynicism are found together. The urban area is more politicized and generates more radical politics than rural India and is more exposed to national issues and the pressures of modernization.'[35]

Vajpeyi has analysed the situation that 'The first phase of the present study was conducted in 1966, only a few months before the fourth general elections in India. The political atmosphere was confusing. Economic policy failures, the governments' credibility gap, administrative corruption, and political fragmentation were making headlines. Besides, constant emphasis upon equality and socialism since the early 1950s had substantially heightened political awareness among rural masses and had excited expectations of tangible gains'.[36]

Frustration among groups was increasingly directed at the political system which symbolised these failures—for if there was one idea that was gaining ground among all sections of Indian opinion, it was the melancholic notion that the most likely victim of continuing administrative and political inertia would be the ruling party. Therefore, it was not the mere exposure to the mass media which contributed to the lack of the citizen's sense of efficacy but the failure of the government in economic and political spheres. The second and the third phase of the study showed similar mass media trends. The 1976 data was collected during the most strict press censorship in the history of post-independent India.[37]

In Uttar Pradesh, it was reported that for the majority of the respondents, particularly in the rural areas, the most effective means of receiving information is oral. Also, the nature of the vernacular press which does not have the resources, expertise and vision of the national or elite press restrict the flow of the communication. Like politics, the communication system in India operates at two levels, on two distinct planes: the local level, and the national level. The local vernacular press is usually oblivious of national issues and does not share the concerns of the elite political culture. This gap itself makes the vast majority of Indians parochial, less cosmopolitan and less eager to change and modernize. The data brings out the crucial role of urbanization in modernization. It is in the urban sample that more participants, highly empathic, and media exposed citizens are found. Cynicism was also reported to be higher among urban respondents than among the rural ones.[38]

The Uttar Pradesh data, while raising some doubts about the relevance of traditional wisdom and models of modernization in the Indian context also supports some theories in the area. In India, a 'deterministic' approach could not spell out the steps towards modernization. The process of modernization in India has to be viewed in the context of India's history, culture and peculiar socialization experiences. India cannot be bound to any specific model or models, 'standard' theories of 'political decay' or 'political modernization'. The Indian model of political modernization has to be based not on entirely new social and political structures and imported criteria of political change, but on a synthesis between a pragmatic approach and traditional Indian social structures and values which would lead to a renewed awareness quickening of traditional identity, its reinterpretation and rejuvenation, and its consolidation in the framework of new institutions and ideas.[39]

Ultimately, Vajpeyi comes to the conclusion that the impact of modernization on India is bound to be mixed, both painful and joyful. Increased political participation, exposure to mass media, rising expectations, and social mobility will put strains on India's political system resulting in unstable political conditions like the post 1967 elections, but this should not tempt the prophets of doom and gloom. India will disappoint them too. Modernity is not new. It is a recurring historical force, a recurring opportunity, as Shakespeare said:

> Which taken at the flood, leads on to fortune;
> Omitted, all the voyage of their life
> Is bound in shallows and in miseries.[40]

The study *Tradition vs Modernity: Women in Nepal and Sri Lanka*[41] by Anuradha and S.D. Muni, may closely be followed by a question as to what socio-cultural differences are accounted in Sri Lanka's island character and Nepal. It is proposed to describe the position of women in these societies. The social, economic and political dimensions of women's role and status are being discussed and compared with men's respective positions.

In Nepalese society, women enjoy a respectable social status and a considerable amount of economic security. Functionally, their role is limited within a family or a community. Their response to the process of modernization has so far not been appreciable. The initiative and leadership of women would depend upon the degree of modern social and political influences.

The spread of education will play a very significant role in this context; the position of women in this respect is lamentable. Women's literacy in Nepal is one of the lowest in the world. The prospects do not seem to be encouraging as the latest education plan does not place any specific emphasis on women's education.

An efficient system of communication can also bring hopeful results towards a larger social awakening and awareness among women. In a small way, the exposure of individuals to the developed societies—through employment in foreign armies, visits for higher education and training, etc. also help families to raise their levels of international awareness. Women do not escape from this process.

In the political sphere, women's organization under the Panchayat system has proved detrimental to the growth of women elites. It has limited the scope and channels of their activities. On the other hand official programmes like family planning make a direct attack on orthodox feminine values and introduce new social dimensions among women. Education among women resulted in their increasing participation in the political processes of the country. The degree of political consciousness is gradually increasing.

The women of Nepal and Sri Lanka enjoyed the same status in their respective traditional societies. At present, they stand at a different footing, except perhaps in their constitutional and legal positions. The differences are clearly evident in their educational attainments, political articulations, initiatives and leadership. The Ceylonese women are better placed in all these fields as compared to their Nepali sisters.

The most important factors that led to progress among Ceylonese women were the British rule in the island, and the process of social and political modernization initiated during that period. In Nepal, the influence of the Indian British Empire was limited to the political sphere alone. Its impact on the kingdom's socio-cultural and economic life was almost negligible.

The gap that stands today in the status and roles of women living at the two ends of the Indian sub-continent is likely to be perpetuated. The rate of socio-cultural modernization in Nepal is much slower than what is required.

Usha Mahajani's paper 'Women's Status and Modernization in Southeast Asia: The Philippines Model',[42] shows that another dimension to the middle and upper class families of India and China that the existence of a nuclear family imposed on women greater participation in outdoor economic occupations.

Mahajani presents the conclusion that the overall picture for women's status in Southeast Asia is not one of straight optimism. They are making great strides in education as opportunities are being made available to them. In the field of business too, they have gained ground but in vital matters of marriage laws their lack of progress is sadly outstanding. Malaysia being a formally Islamic country, any legislation abolishing polygyny and giving equal property rights to women would not even be considered. In Indonesia the betrayal of women is particularly deplorable. Nowhere else in Southeast Asia except in Vietnam have women done so much for the cause of freedom and nowhere else have they launched such a well organised, universal feminist, agitation for marriage reforms as in Indonesia. It is a clear-cut case of the stubborn refusal of men to give up the privilege conferred upon them by Islam. In 1973, the Indonesian Parliament passed a law permitting polygamy with endorsement by the court in cases where the wife "is unable to perform her duties as a wife", is physically disabled or has an incurable disease, or "is unable to bear offspring". Under the law, mutual consent is required for polygyny "except where it is impossible to obtain the wife's consent". The minimum age of marriage for girls is 16 years but a court dispensation can be obtained, where an earlier marriage is considered necessary. Thus, the Suharto government has dealt a decisive blow to the cause of women's emancipation. Overall prospects for raising women's status and their educational and career opportunities in Asia are less bright today than before.

Women have a major political role to play in a democratic set-up (not all but at least in some) and under left-wing or communist politics. But military dictatorship is a peculiarly male chauvinist phenomenon. Not surprisingly, even Indonesian women, highly politicized during the Suharto period both before and after independence, have no place of influence or prominence under General Suharto's military rule. On the other hand, Southeast Asia has produced a peculiar phenomenon of female power behind the throne—but generally associated with scandals of corruption as in the Philippines (under Marcos), Cambodia (under Sihanouk), Indonesia (under Suharto) and South Vietnam (under Diem). This must be remarked as the greatest perversion of the ancient role of royal women in Southeast Asia.

The study by K.N. Jha appeared in the book, *Women Towards Modernization*.[43] This study is a systematic investigation into the indices of modernity found in the urban community life in Patna (Bihar). The study does not cover the whole city population. It is confined to a particular section of people. The universe under study is a group of college and university lady teachers residing and working in Patna.

Referring to Jha's study, the eminent Indian sociologist, Yogendra Singh remarks: "But a majority of studies employ a structural model of analysis for the treatment of women's roles and status in society (M.N. Srinivas: 1978; .... K.N. Jha: 1985; ..)."[44] Further Yogendra Singh remarks: "Other studies have analysed aspects of role conflict among women in different domains of responsibilities (K. Chakravarti: 1978; K.N. Jha: 1985; .....)."[45]

Kumud Ranjan writes that "K.N. Jha (1985) in his study of the college and university lady teachers residing and working in Patna has made an attempt to find out the impact of modernization in the working women who were hitherto rooted in the exploitative structures of male-dominated society. It has been found that a rational and modern outlook is becoming increasingly apparent among women. Their approaches towards marriage, interpersonal relationship in the family and kinship network are changing too. The women are changing their habits, manners and ways of life which have become much different from the traditional patterns. They are assuringly heading towards a positive goal without any compromise with the existing social restrictions and reservations. The picture is happy indeed."[46]

Referring to the study, Saraswati Mishra writes: "As Jha (1985) has stated, women also advanced towards modernization. Consequently, traditional blind faiths and narrow-mindedness in women were left behind and they became increasingly aware of their interests. Today, they have moved to protest against atrocities on them and they have got its benefits also. Direct or indirect information about other developed countries has helped them to become more aware of their interests and now they are active in the direction of establishing this fact that they are not inferior to men in any point of view and they can do all those jobs properly which were being considered limited only up to the jurisdiction of men."[47]

"Jha has presented the conclusion that college and university women teachers are exposed to a number of modern forces and factors. A process of tradition-modernity continuum exists and the women are dominantly rational and modern in their outlook and actual behaviour, though the actual practice is slightly lagging behind the actual ideas and attitudes."[48]

A number of sociologists and social scientists have studied, explained and analysed the process of modernization in India and its relation to women. Jamila Brijbhushan,[49] M. Chaki-Sircar,[50] Bipin Chandra,[51] D.A. Chekki,[52] Suma Chitnis,[53] A.R. Desai,[54] Neera Desai and V. Patel,[55] S.C. Dube,[56] D. Jain,[57] Kala Rani,[58] M. Mies,[59] R.N. Saksena,[60] K.L. Sharma,[61] Karuna Channa,[62] Sushila Jain,[63] Saraswati Mishra,[64] Kumud Ranjan,[65] Indu Prakash Singh,[66] Dipankar Gupta,[67] Maitrayee Chaudhuri,[68] Nilika Mehrotra,[69] Vinita Singh and Kali Nath Jha[70] are prominent among them.

The study by Sushila Jain has come through the book, *Muslims and Modernization*. Jain has explained that the Muslim community in India can best be seen in the context of a number of minority groups struggling to preserve their respective identities even as they compete for the rewards of economic development. What sets it apart is its unique historical experience. Jain writes: "My interest is primarily in exploring the impact of these social, political and economic changes in the Muslim community and on the perception of these Muslims of their status, role and values as members of families, the Muslim community and the larger and more heterogeneous Indian community."

The study attempts to identify the traditional social structure of Islam. It attempts to identify historical factors which made the modernizing process in the Muslim community lack both unity and cohesion. It further examines the effect this had on the Muslims and on the community's pre-partition (1947) development. It deals with the period after 1947, which is characterized by the national focus on economic development and modernization. It examines whether the national drive for modernization stimulated the desire in the Muslim community for economic progress and modernization. It also deals with the problem, i.e., definition of the concept used and the research design. The study also deals with the nature and extent of modernization in the institutional complex (e.g., of family and marriage). The study highlights the degree of secularization and religion amongst the Muslim respondents and it is concerned with the analysis of the changing aspirations and values of the Muslims. This inquiry was directed at assessing the extent to which occupational and educational aspirations were limited by the ascribed status, and to what extent their achieved status has been affected by the advent of industrialization, economic development and modern education. It probes the direction and resolution of their desire for change in their value system. The study explains the role and the status of Muslim women, their political awareness, political involvement and political orientation of the male respondents studied in the Muslim community in Jaipur. Jain further writes that "in short the underlying question under consideration was, given the shortcomings of their ascribed status, to what extent the achieved status is being affected and to what extent post independence efforts at economic development and modernization have helped or hindered this process of modernization in this community". Jain further writes: "As far as the modernization of Muslims in Jaipur city is concerned, we find a growing trend that traditional role structures are giving way to modern ones. But persons following these roles often retain categorical values of tradition instead of those of modernity. Generally, ritual order and religion which are essentially based on categorical values of a traditional nature do not show evidence of decline, nor is there an easy possibility of their disappearance in the near future. The categorical values can hardly be falsified by scientific proof and hence the spread of science may not logically lead to obsolescence of traditional categorical values. Hence, particularistic growth patterns of modernization seem to be more credible than universalistic form of its development. Further course of modernization in this community would depend much on the manner in which the tensions between the past and the contemporary would be resolved as modernization would gather momentum."[71]

Dipankar Gupta's contribution 'Mistaken Modernity' as reviewed in *The Economist*, which Dipankar Gupta contends, justly, is that India's fascination with western gadgetry and lifestyle has not brought modernity. Gupta writes that modernity entails adhering to universal norms, upholding individual rights, making the state accountable. His book pleads with India to put modernization in place of 'westoxication'.[72] This book is reviewed in *Deccan Herald*, thus: 'This book ... stands testimony to the importance of bringing in academic/sociological insights into current debates.. (An) immensely readable book.[73]

Gupta is of the view that "the ideas in this book grew out of my writings in the popular press. There is a tendency among academics to look down upon journalistic pieces, and to some extent this position is probably justified. However, I think this dismissive attitude towards journalism exists probably because academics find it very difficult to write in a popular language, and to translate their sophisticated ideas in a fashion that would appeal to the lay person."

Gupta writes: "I have written this book in a style that should appeal to non-academics, but that does not in any way diminish my indebtedness to scholarly contributions, particularly in sociology and anthropology. I try not to give too much ostensible evidence of this (I have kept my bibliographical references to the minimum), but on issues like hygiene, religion, the middle class, politics of patronage, and indeed, on the larger theme of modernity, I have been deeply influenced by academic works on these subjects."

Gupta further writes: "I chose to write on modernity, or rather, on India's mistaken modernity, because of the way people rather loosely associate it with symbols of technological progress, such as cars, gadgets, frequent travels abroad, and so forth. I have found such understandings of modernity fairly offensive whether one goes to a hospital or a school, or participates in politics, there is no escaping the fact that mode of relations among people in our country is still not modern. Family connections, privileges of caste and status, as well as the willingness to break every law in the book, characterise our social relations very deeply."[74]

Gupta argued that true modernity is about how people relate to other people, and likewise, true ethics is all about a concern with 'others' as equal citizens. Modernity is an attitude which represents universalistic norms, where the dignity of an individual as a citizen is inviolable and where one's achievement counts far more than family background and connections. Once modernity is understood in this fashion, it appears that India still has a long distance to go.[75]

Gupta explains that modernity has been misrecognised in India because of the tendency to equate it with technology and with other contemporary artefacts. The possession of modern technology, however, does not always signal modernity. Modernity has to do with attitudes, especially those that come into play in social relations. A modern society is one in which at least the following characteristics must be present:

— Dignity of the individual;
— Adherence to universalistic norms;
— Elevation of individual achievement over privileges or disprivileges of birth;
— Accountability in public life.

Once these attributes are in place, it does not really matter if there is high-level technology, superfast transit systems, or consumerism. Generally speaking, technology and consumerism are consequences of the four characteristics of modernization listed above, and do not by themselves constitute modernity.[76]

Gupta has explained that "in India, we have not paid attention to the mainsprings of modernity, but have been quick to declare certain sectors as modern because of their acquisition of artefacts and technology. This has led to frequent complaints against modernity, especially when egregious offences are committed in contemporary locales or their perpetrators are those who were mistakenly seen as modern because they possessed expensive material objects. Thus, sexual harassment, violence in public places, dowry deaths and a host of other fairly uncivilised forms of conduct get posted as modern. They are carry-overs of attitudes from the past. The abuse of women, the demonstration of family connections and the refusal to abide by norms are actually traditional attributes. But if these are manifest today in a bar, a hotel or in a university, chances are that people would shake their heads and lament on the course that modernity has brought upon us.

An analysis of contemporary India reveals that while there has been a definite move from tradition, what we see around us is not yet modern. If the clock were to stop here, the final diagnosis would, or rather should, declare India as still unmodern. Modernity always comes in baby steps, more so in a country like India where tradition was not only deeply entrenched but also highly elaborated in all walks of life. Traditional India was perhaps the most stratified society in the world, as it ritually sanctioned the separation among human beings on the basis of caste in such fine detail.

The effects of this can be felt even today in India. While industrialization has indeed made a difference and so has democratic politics, there is still a long way to go. This is because the advances of industrialization and politics have largely been concerned with members of the traditional elite. In some cases, where these traditional elites have been displaced, the new ruling class has not heralded a modern outlook, but has instead adopted the values of its predecessors. Consequently, the old elite classes have not been pressured in any significant way.

Modernity cannot be held up forever, but it can take a very long time. In countries like India, an additional and concerted push is required to further its progress. This can happen, in part, at the conscious level, once we realise what modernity is all about and who its friends and enemies are.

It is not as if modernity is an exercise in will power alone. In fact, a modern attitude develops not so much because people choose to adopt it but rather because little scope for choice in this matter. The social conditions that favour and encourage modernity must be paid attention to. If modernity implies the four features we mentioned earlier the only way they have a reasonable chance of coming into existence is when significant numbers from the lower classes graduate to the level of the middle class and when the economic structure allows for a great degree of social mobility.

Obviously, for all this to happen industrialization is absolutely essential. But what has often been overlooked is that industrialization is a necessary but not sufficient condition for modernity. Generations may live and die by factory stacks, conveyor belts and rapid wheels, and yet not experience true modernity. It is at this point that a heightened self-consciousness of what modernity really is can act as a catalyst to hasten the process."[77]

Gupta has further explained that it is often easily overlooked that developed modernity is characterised by an attitude of equality with, and respect for, others. It is not as if in a modern society all are actually equal. Yet, in spite of the many differences that exist among people, modernity demands a baseline similarity so that people can live with dignity and can realistically avail themselves of opportunities to better their conditions of existence. It is on this bedrock of equality that other differences and inequalities can be added on. But the foundational equality cannot be compromised for it is on this that claims of citizenship are made in modern societies. In traditional orders, there were rulers and subjects but no citizens.

Thus, modernity can only come into being when 'intersubjectivity' is a central concern. But intersubjectivity does not come easily. Intersubjectivity is about being able to participate in one another's lives and "share in one another's fate".[78] Even if we are located at structurally different points in terms of our occupations and skills, the distance should not be of the kind that we cannot imagine what it is like to be in some one else's shoes. Intersubjectivity thus arouses the quality of empathy. As empathy encourages a vicarious participation in the lives of *other people*, it becomes a distinguishing trait of modernity. This and other attributes of a modern attitude help in the realisation of substantive (not just legal) citizenship.

But, in India today, it is still very difficult to work up any enthusiasm for projects which have a public utility in mind. The sense that as citizens we share a common public space, implying thereby that in some very significant ways we are responsible for one another's well-being, has found very few takers in India. The better-off and seemingly more 'modern' sectors are the most reluctant to actively participate as citizens for that would imply that they must treat the less privileged with greater respect. This is a sad fact which the Indian elite are not willing to fully recognise as that would take the mantle of modernity away from them.

Developed modernity is then characterised by a certain distinctive attitude that comes into effect on our relations with other people. Have we not all seen or known of ultramodern hospitals where doctors and administrators treat patients and subordinate staff, including nurses, as clear unequals? It is also widely accepted that there are many business houses in India which have travelled far down the road of advanced technology and yet decision-making within the firm is still run on the old tycoon principle. In such cases, not only is the management not separated from ownership, but enterprise itself is held back as communications flow only from the top down. Further, even in corporate business, as elsewhere, connections matter more than universal principles of justice and fair play. There is nothing that money and good connections cannot fix. The patronage network thus tends to survive and do rather well even in the so-called advanced sectors of the economy.[79] In this way, Dipankar Gupta has contributed his valuable viewpoint and brings sociological insights into current debates.

In the present age of globalization, social relations are changing. Due to the revolution in communication, caste and polity, ethnic identity, middle class phenomenon, relations between local and global culture, migration of tribal women, Indian diaspora and women's emancipation have emerged as questions. In the words of Yogendra Singh, "The strength of sociology as a discipline lies in its ability to unravel the mysteries of the surface social phenomena or events in their deeper structural context as a whole. In this respect, the sociological reasoning takes into account not only the immediate present, but also the past of a social event."[80]

Notes

1. Daniel Lerner, *The Passing of Traditional Society: Modernizing the Middle East*, Preface, pp. VIII-IX, New York: The Free Press, 1966.
2. Ibid., p. IX.
3. Ibid.
4. Ibid., p. 466.
5. S.S. Mathur, *A Sociological Approach to Indian Education*, Vinod Pustak Mandir, Agra, 1997, p. 76.
6. Edward Shils, *The Intellectual Between Tradition and Modernity: The Indian Situation*, The Huge: Mouton, 1961, pp. 110-12.
7. Yogendra Singh, *Essays on Modernization in India*, Manohar, New Delhi, 1978, pp. 78-79.
8. Ibid., pp. 79-80.
9. Ibid., pp. 86-87.
10. Ibid., pp. 87-88.
11. Ibid., p. 93.
12. Ibid., p. 120.
13. Promilla Kapur, "Studies of Urban Women in India", in *Family and Social Change in Modern India* by Giriraj Gupta (ed.) (Main Currents in Indian Sociology-II), Vikas, New Delhi, 1976.
14. K.T. Merchant, *Changing Views on Marriage and the Family*, B.G. Paul and Company, Madras, 1935.
15. Margaret L. Cormack, *The Hindu Women*, Columbia University Press, 1953.

    —, *She who rides a Peacock*, Asia Publishing House, Bombay, 1961.
16. B.V. Shah, *Social Change and College Students of Gujarat*, M.S. University of Baroda, Baroda, 1964.
17. B.K. Jha, *A Study of Habits of Boys and Girls of Higher Secondary Schools in Raipur Town*, M.Ed. Thesis, Sagar University, Sagar, 1964.
18. A. Mathew, "Expectations of College Students regarding their Marriage", *Social Welfare*, 12 (March), 1966, pp. 46-52.
19. G.C. Hallen, "Attitudes of Educated Youth Towards Marriage", *Social Welfare*, 12 (February), 1966, pp. 9-10.
20. P.C. Mitra, "Experiments in Middle Class Habits and Preferences", *Indian Journal of Psychology*, 19, 1944, pp. 21-31.
21. Promilla Kapur, op. cit.
22. Ibid., pp. 78-79.

23. Rama Mehta, *The Western Educated Hindu Women*, Asia Publishing House, Bombay, 1970.
24. Promilla Kapur, op. cit.
25. Ibid., pp. 78-79.
26. YWCA of India, *The Educated Woman in Indian Society*, Tata McGraw Hill Publishing Co., New Delhi, 1971.
27. Promilla Kapur, op. cit.
28. Rhoda L. Goldstein, *Indian Women in Transition: A Bangalore Case Study*, Metuchen, New Jersey: The Scarecrow Press, 1972.
29. Promilla Kapur, op. cit.
30. Promilla Kapur, *Love, Marriage and Sex*, Vikas, New Delhi, 1973.
31. Promilla Kapur, "Studies of Urban Women in India", in *Family and Social Change in Modern India*, (II), by Giriraj Gupta (ed.), Vikas, New Delhi, 1976.
32. S.K. Kuthiala, *From Tradition to Modernity*, Abhinav Publications, New Delhi, 1973.
33. Ibid., Preface, p. X.
34. D.K. Vajpeyi, *Modernization and Social Change in India*, Manohar, New Delhi, 1979.
35. Ibid., p. 260.
36. Ibid.
37. Ibid., p. 261.
38. Ibid., p. 263.
39. Ibid., p. 264.
40. Ibid., pp. 264-65.
41. Anuradha and S.D. Muni, "Tradition vs Modernity: Women in Nepal", in *Women of the World* by Urmilla Phadnis and Indira Malani (eds.), Vikas, New Delhi, 1978.
42. Usha Mahajani, "Women's Status and Modernization in South East Asia: The Philippines Model", in *Women of the World* by Urmilla Phadnis and Indira Malani (eds.), Vikas, New Delhi, 1978.
43. K.N. Jha, *Women Towards Modernization*, Janki Prakashan, Patna, 1985.
44. Yogendra Singh, *Indian Sociology: Social Conditioning and Emerging Concerns*, Vistaar Publications, New Delhi, 1986, p. 89.
45. Ibid., p. 91.
46. Kumud Ranjan, *Women and Modern Occupation in India*, Chug Publications, Allahabad, 1993, p. 18.

47. Saraswati Mishra, *Status of Indian Women*, Gyan Publishing House, New Delhi, 2002, p. 158.
48. K.N. Jha, op. cit., p. 120.
49. Jamila Brijbhushan, *Muslim Women: In Purdah and Out of It*, Vikas, New Delhi.
50. M. Chaki-Sircar, *Feminism in a Traditional Society: Women of the Manipur Valley*, Shakti Books, Vikas, New Delhi, 1984.
51. Bipin Chandra, 1970, "Colonialism and Modernization". Paper presented at the 32nd Indian History Congress, Jabalpur, December 1970.
52. D.A. Chekki, *Modernization and Kin Network*, Leiden: E.J. Brill, 1974.
53. Suma Chitnis, "The Teacher's Role in the College System", unpublished Ph.D thesis, Tata Institute of Social Sciences, Bombay, 1973.
54. A.R. Desai, *Essays on Modernization of Underdeveloped Societies* (ed.), Thacker: Bombay, 2V, 1971.
55. Neera Desai and Patel, *Indian Women: Change and Challenge in the International Decade 1975-85*, Popular Prakashan, Bombay, 1985.
56. S.C. Dube, *Contemporary India and its Modernization*, Vikas Publishing House, New Delhi, 1973.
57. D. Jain, *Indian Women: Today and Tomorrow*, Nehru Memorial Museum and Library, New Delhi, 1982.
58. Kala Rani, *Role Conflict in Working Women*, Chetna Publications, New Delhi, 1976.
59. M. Mies, *Indian Women and Patriarchy: Conflicts and Dilemmas of Students and Working Women*, Concept Publishing Company, New Delhi, 1980.
60. R.N. Saksena, "Modernization and Development: Trends in India", *Sociological Bulletin*, 21(2), 1972, pp. 91-102.
61. K.L. Sharma, "Modernization and Rural Stratification: An Application at the Micro-level", *Economic and Political Weekly*, 5(37), 1970, pp. 1537-43.
62. Karuna Channa, *Socialization, Education and Women: Exploration in Gender Identity*, (ed.), Orient Longman Ltd., Hyderabad, 1988.
63. Sushila Jain, *Muslims and Modernization: A Study of Their Changing Role Structure and Norms in an Urban Setting*, Rawat Publications, Jaipur and New Delhi, 1986.
64. Saraswati Mishra, op. cit.
65. Kumud Ranjan, op. cit.

66. Indu Prakash Singh, *Indian Women: The Captured Beings*, Intellectual Publishing House, New Delhi, 1990.
67. Dipankar Gupta, *Mistaken Modernity India Between Worlds*, Harper Collins Publishers India, 2000.
68. Maitrayee Chaudhuri, "Gender in the Making of the Indian Nation-State", *Sociological Bulletin*, Vol. 48(1-2), March-September 1999.

    —, *Feminism in India*, Kali for Women, New Delhi, 2004.
69. Nilika Mehrotra, "Grassroots Women Activism: A Case Study from Delhi", *Indian Anthropologist*, Vol. 27 (2), December 1997.

    —, "Understanding Feminism in a Local Context", *Indian Anthropologist*, Vol. 31(1), June-December 2001.

    —, "Perceiving Feminism: Some Local Responses", *Sociological Bulletin*, Vol. 51(1), March 2002.
70. Vinita Singh and Kali Nath Jha, "Emerging Professionals: Saleswomen in Ranchi". Paper presented in the 'XXIX All India Sociological Conference', Udaipur, December 21-23, 2003.

    —, "Process of Globalization: A Study of Tribal Women Students in Ranchi". Paper presented in the Golden Jubilee Seminar on 'Anthropology and the Challenge of Development in Jharkhand', Department of Anthropology, Ranchi University, Ranchi and Anthropological Survey of India, January 19-21, 2004.

    —, "Migration of Tribal Women from Jharkhand: The Price of Development". Paper presented in the National Seminar on 'Tribes, State Policies and NGOs', organized by Indian Anthropological Association, New Delhi, March 26-27, 2004.
71. Sushila Jain, op. cit.
72. Dipankar Gupta, op. cit., p. I.
73. Ibid., p. II.
74. Ibid., p. IX-X.
75. Ibid., p. X.
76. Ibid., p. 2.
77. Ibid., pp. 2-4.
78. Rawls, *A Theory of Justice*, Cambridge, Massachusetts: The Belknep Press of Harvard University, 1971.
79. Gupta, Dipankar Gupta, op. cit., pp. 5-6.
80. Yogendra Singh, *Culture Change in India: Identity and Globalization*, Rawat Publications, Jaipur and New Delhi, 2000, p. 253.

4

Family: Power and Decision-Making

In Indian society, the most important institutions are religious traditions, lineage system, familial organization and marriage which provide a moral basis to the rights and duties of men and women. All these institutions have traditionally determined a four-layered role and status order for women, i.e., as daughter, wife, housewife and mother through which the woman's world got restricted to the family. Even in the family, she became subordinate to men and occupied a secondary place.[1]

In India, in its south-west and north-west regions, the matrilineal system is practised, in which lineage tradition is accepted from the women's side but in the women's family, power still remains in the hands of a man, especially in the higher caste group where the wife remains engaged inside the house and the husband goes out of the house for work. An overwhelming majority of Indian people follow the patrilineal system of lineage order. Man advances the lineage and work of the family. At the time of marriage, the daughter leaves the family and lineage of her father and joins the family and lineage of her husband. This affects the status of women, which is related to her legal rights also. Some religious duties of the family can be performed only by a son owing to the social cultural compulsion of the daughter's marriage. The girl has been considered a burden, especially because the parents spend money on her rearing, education and health, without any expectation of financial assistance of any sort, from her and due to this reason only in these matters and right of property, differentiation has been practised between the man and the woman. The cultural concept that the role of women is only secondary, i.e., of assistant, is related with this tendency directly and it is the outcome of mainly the patrilineal system and the wife's living in the husband's residence.[2]

The joint family organization is a combination of those patrilineal male relatives who have equal rights on property and the total expenditure on them comes from the same source; who live in the same house and eat food cooked from the same fire place. It is expected from a woman that after marriage she should mould herself according to her in-laws' household. Owing to the process of socialization starting from childhood, after the time of marriage she develops a sense of belonging towards the new family. With the passage of time this feeling of oneness or affinity keeps on strengthening. She is kept under strict control as a daughter-in-law. In the decision-taking on any issue, she has either very little or no say and she remains in subordination to her mother-in-law. Her status in the family depends upon her husband's contribution in the household economy. In the higher and middle class her status depends even on the dowry brought by her at the time of marriage as well as the financial benefits got from the parental family from time to time. In the middle class, the mother of grown-up children gets respect and privileges and she gets the rights of taking decisions also. Although women perform only a marginal role in decision-taking, generally privileges of the mother, which convert daughter-in-law into a maid servant, get diminished along with old age and widowhood or due to increased importance of daughter-in-law as the wife of a bread earner for the family and mother of growing-up children. In north India, customs of using a veil in front of husband's relatives and touching their feet by the wife are quite prevalent.

In the patrilineal society, after marriage, a woman gets transferred from her birth lineage to her husband's birth lineage. For girls, marriages arranged at an early age are considered most desirable because this concept is connected with the importance of protection of virginity, restriction of marriage in the same lineage and proper adjustment in the husband's house.[3]

Sex Role

Bernice Lott writes: "A mother trains her daughter for her roles as housewife and rearing of children very easily by making her an assistant in all the household jobs."[4] Mishra has expressed her views that apart from this, through observation of mothers performance of different roles, daughter herself internalizes the ideas regarding expected behaviour and utilizes them in future.[5] Chanana has stated that, while the girls are made an expert of the household affairs before her marriage, the boy is trained and prepared for earning livelihood by giving him opportunities of experiencing the outside world through getting the outside jobs done by him.[6] In this way, due to sex difference, the girls and boys are socialized for different roles mainly by the family, although the process of socialization goes on throughout life, for accommodation of a person according to changed circumstances. But, in every situation, there is division of labour between the man and the woman.[7]

During the process of socialization, differentiation between the boy and the girl is justified on different bases. One more basis for differentiation in socialization of both the sexes is psychological. Under this, it is considered that they are inferior to men.[8] Chanana remarks: "In comparison to men they have less intellectual capabilities, logical mind, perception and farsightedness. By nature they are imaginative, emotional, impulsive and cowardly. They get influenced by others very easily and they themselves are unable to think and act rationally. It is thought that they do not have the ability to take important decisions, hence the responsibility of functions having long term effects, should not be handed over to them, because they cannot handle it properly. Therefore, the functions needing more mental ability should be performed by men only. If the assistance of women is required it can be taken by men in order to complete the task. Owing to this reason, right from the beginning women are taught to include the virtues of adjustment, obedience, subordination, submissiveness, dedication, etc., in their personalities. They internalize the negative self image originated by socialization."[9] Mishra has expressed her views regarding the expected roles of women. One stream of thought directs them to perform household jobs and particular outside jobs different from men, by pointing out their particular biological structure as being responsible for their specific psychological composition being different from men.[10]

Decision-Making

In any group, the status of its members gets expressed to a great extent by their rights of taking decisions regarding themselves and the whole group. In the family, various decisions are required to be taken regarding daily affairs like maintenance of the house, the lifestyle of members, food, relations with outside people, and regarding particular occasional acts having far-reaching effects such as the financial budget of the family, purchase of things to be used for a long time, buying and selling of immovable property, education, profession and marriages of children, etc. Generally, in a group, the power of decision-taking depends on a person's sex, age, education and income. An aged, experienced, educated and financially sound person gets the leadership of the group automatically.[11]

The traditional joint family was marked by an authoritarian family set up. A historical system of authority was distinctly specified. In this hierarchy, age sequence and male domination were most effective ascriptive criteria. The older generation had authority over the younger generation. The eldest male member was the acknowledged head of the family. His authority was absolute. Since authority was vested in him, he made all the important decisions, with or without consultation of other adult members in the family. His decision was binding and final. The female member was allotted a subordinate position to man. She had to serve her husband and the family members.[12]

Due to growth of industrialization, urbanization, the process of modernization and globalization, the relations to the others and the traditional pattern of authority have changed. Sood writes: "As the women have started taking up jobs, it is expected that relatively, it will also affect traditional power structure in the family. When a woman works, she presumably increases her ability to sanction or control, because of the financial contribution she makes to the family. Especially, the modern educated woman wants her say to be implemented in the family affairs. She wants to involve herself in decisions, at least regarding children's education, shopping, budgeting and financial matters. Hence, her status improves both with respect to her expected and actual power and authority."[13]

For our purpose, power is defined as the ability which a person has in evolving the process of decision-making. Theoretically speaking, power varies with variations or change in the ability to control others. To quote Max Weber, "power means the opportunity, no matter on what basis, of enforcing one's own will in the context of a social relationship".[14] Power and authority of women would increase with their increased participation in gainful economic and occupational pursuits outside their homes. Conversely, if they continue to remain confined to their homes mainly as housewives, they are likely to remain under the spell of male-domination. However, it is not that all women who are employed have attained equality with men and vice-versa.

In a family a suggestion such as "what ought to be done" is the usual way of originating a consensus about a decision to be taken. Hence, the number of initial suggestions by either sex becomes the basis of family decisions. This process indicates the participation of members in evolving a consensus. If control of resources determines power in the family, then the average working women and particularly those engaged in higher occupations have a bigger say than the women engaged in lower occupations. In other words, the higher the economic level, the greater will be the power to decide important matters regarding self as well as family, and the higher will be the level of self-esteem.[15]

Sood writes: "By self-esteem we mean the estimation that an individual reaches and maintains regarding his personal work. It refers to the positive or negative orientation towards one's self. The individual constantly evaluates himself in the context of his society and fellowmen. These evaluations are derived from the values of the significant others... This exercise is a sort of constructing a mirror, in which an individual sees his self-image. Thus, self-esteem is a dynamic aspect of self-image and also its most significant index. This self-definition expresses a judgement of approval about overall ability and worth. Self-esteem, so defined, is a subjective appraisal by an individual of his own values as a human being."[16]

In this way, in order to evaluate the pattern of power relations in the families of highly educated women, it is essential to assess the influence of the various members of their families in important decisions. It was difficult to get a complete record of all the decisions; however, information was collected regarding some aspects, namely, money matters, key decisions and other important decisions regarding self as well as family.

Utilization of Money Earned by Self

Development expenditure is expressive of creative home making because it provides each member of the family with what he or she needs for education, recreation and individual development. The supreme value of good health should be the guiding factor behind expenditure on food, clothes and shelter. There are, however, other expenses necessary for the maintenance of good health such as vacations and many other forms of recreation. Expenses are, therefore, influenced by travel, games, theatres, music and musical instruments. Development expenditures also include cost of books and magazines, hospitality and gifts and individual allowances for each member of the family.

Whether earning or not, a woman is a part and parcel of a family. Whether it is the family of her parents, or that of her husband, the decision-making on how her earnings are to be spent may rest jointly with wife and husband or daughter and father, or it may be invested only in the husband or the father in his capacity as the head of the family, or it may rest with employed women or unemployed women themselves.[17]

The study reveals that for 70 percent highly educated women and majority of them with lower economic status, who continued to follow traditional patterns of living, the decisions rest entirely on their husbands or parents. But 27.5 percent highly educated women control their self-earned money, because they are in the higher economic group and they have higher educational and economic status. Only 2.5 percent women, who continued to follow dominantly traditional patterns of living and decision-making, are entirely dependent on their families.

Family Budgeting

In the families of 84 percent of highly educated women, who have moderate decision-making power, most of the decisions are taken jointly by the family members. The majority of women have a minimal role in decision-making. Only 15 percent of women have the power to decide regarding the family budgeting. One percent of women have no role in decision-making. But it is the indication of higher status of women in comparison to the past. Now, the role of women in family structure is changing.

Investments and Savings

Major investments and savings for the family is one of the most important items of decision-making in the family. In the case of

83.5 percent of the highly educated women, the investments and savings are controlled by both, women and husband/ parents. As it is clear, in majority of the cases irrespective of occupational status, joint decision-making regarding major investments and savings is the general practice. But, in the case of 16 percent women, they are themselves responsible for investments and savings. Only in the case of 0.5 percent of the highly educated women, they are not included in decision-making regarding investments and savings.

Control over Family Income

As per to Sood's analysis, the status of women in the family is the extent of their power in the management of the economic resources of the family. There was no economic function assigned to women. Employment of women would have contributed to some changes in the traditional norms regarding decision-making and in the increase in women's power in the decision-making in the family and hence in their status. A woman's contribution to the family income would enable her to have a say in the spending of the income and she would receive greater cooperation and respect from other family members.

However, earning money and its contribution to the family income, may not necessarily increase a woman's status, nor may the actual decision-making contribute to change in the status unless she enjoys real power in managing the family resources, namely spending income.

Thus, the question essentially is how far the employment of women really helps to bring about a change in the economic power structure of a family in favour of women. The hypothesis here is that employment of women outside their homes increases their status and power in the family.

The assumption is that money is an important basis of economic power and control over the spending of money leads to overall power of the people. An independent basis of earning would enable the working women to exert influence on the male members of the family. The greater social interaction as a result of working outside may lead to an increase in the development of social skills and self confidence which may result in the use of money more carefully and intelligently.[18]

The study reveals that 16 percent of the women enjoy maximum freedom regarding spending family income. Whereas 83.5 percent of women enjoy moderate decision-making, only 0.5 percent of the women have the lowest decision-making power. In the case of women belonging to lower income group families, the husband/in-laws have control over the working wife's income.

Purchase of Consumer Goods

Autonomy in purchasing of consumer goods is very important to evaluate the power of decision-making and economic status in the family. About 65 percent women have the autonomy to purchase consumer goods of their own choice. In the case of 32.5 percent of the women, the consumer goods are purchased with the consent of their husbands or parents, whereas 2.5 percent women, have no freedom to purchase consumer goods.

Schooling and Career of Children

There are some important areas where decisions are most meaningful. Who takes such decisions determines the source of authority in the family. Both father and mother are needed as the child's companions and as his interpreters of life. The study shows that a majority of 84 percent families follow the consent of both husband and wife on this vital issue. Around 15 percent women are taking decisions at their own cost, whereas only one percent of the women are neglected by their husbands and other members of the family.

Decisions Regarding Marriage

The study reveals that out of 175 (87.5%) married women, only 15 women (7.5%) took decisions regarding marriage by themselves, whereas 25 unmarried women (12.5%) supported marriage of their own choice. Significantly, 80 percent of the women left this decision regarding marriage for their parents to take on their behalf.

Resentment

About 40 percent women resented the power gained by their husbands or fathers whereas the majority of 60 percent women did not resent the power gained by their husbands or fathers. It is but natural for a daughter to resent the power gained by her father or for the wife to resent the power gained by her husband when the power is used unilaterally or indiscriminately, and not shared with her as a grown-up earning hand.

Higher educational and economic status of women will result in better authority for women within the family. It will also result in their having better access to taking important decisions related to money matters. Due to new roles, women today have a better say in the decision making structure of the family and status as compared to women in the past. Thus, the higher the economic status of women, the greater is her say in the family decisions.

Notes

1. Shashi Jain, *Status and Role Perception of Middle Class Women*, Puja Publications, New Delhi, 1988.
2. Saraswati Mishra, *Status of Indian Women*, Gyan Publishing House, New Delhi, 2002, pp. 107-8.
3. Ibid., pp. 108-9.
4. Lott Bernice, *Becoming a Woman (The Socialization of Gender)*, Charles C. Thomas, Illinois, USA, 1981.
5. Saraswati Mishra, *op. cit.*, p. 110.
6. Karuna Chanana (ed.), *Socialization, Education and Women: Exploration in Gender Identity*, Orient Longman Ltd., 1988.
7. Saraswati Mishra, *op. cit.*, p. 110.

8. Ibid., p. 111.
9. Karuna Chanana, *op. cit.*
10. Saraswati Mishra, *op. cit.*, p. 113.
11. Ibid., p. 118.
12. Rita Sood, *Changing Status and Adjustment of Women*, Manak Publications Pvt. Ltd., Delhi and Jaipur, 1991, pp. 75-76.
13. Ibid., pp. 76-77.
14. Max Weber, *Essays in Sociology*, by H.H. Girth and C.W. Mills (eds.), New York: Oxford University Press, 1946, p. 180.
15. Rita Sood, *op. cit.*, p. 77.
16. Ibid., pp. 77-78.
17. Ibid., pp. 79-80.
18. Ibid., pp. 83-84.

5

Role: Adjustment and Attitude

Yogendra Singh has expounded: "Modernization could be analysed structurally, in terms of roles and role sets, and culturally, in terms of values and ideologies. What such studies often neglected is that roles and values are not fully autonomous; nor is the autonomy between structure and culture absolute. Role is defined as a "patterned sequence of learned action or deeds performed by a person in an interaction situation" (Sarbin, 1959: 225). Learning evidently implies internalization of values and their incorporation into the system of behaviour. The motivational element in action is thus invariably mediated by values. Thus, role embodies culture."[1]

Yogendra Singh further writes: "Our assumption is that, in an empirical formulation of modernization, the nature of roles and role-structures could be derived from an analysis of interdependent variables which may be related to elements in the motivational structure (e.g., aspiration and morale), and the system of values (e.g., commitment, universalism, authoritarianism) and relevant to modernization. Instead of observing directly, the role structures could thus be hypothetically deduced from the combination of a selected number of motivational and cultural variables. These variables are expected to have mutually reinforcing relationships in the composite process that is modernization: It sets off adaptive or innovative changes, through the growth of new systems of values and ideologies and through differentiation of role structures.

In the process, however, if new structural foci emerge without the growth of corresponding value systems, strains and tensions are logically expected to emerge in the functioning of the system. Developing countries in Asia now have a wide array of modernising structures which, on the one hand, contribute to modernization and, on the other, also generate tensions and crises during the transition from tradition to modernity. The symptoms of these crises, of course, differ in accordance with the nature of the structures, especially depending on whether they are local or regional or have a macro-level spread of networks".[2]

Role, viewed in the context of functionality, can be considered to be a characteristic of actions expected from an individual occupying some position in the social network. In the other words role is a set of functions attached to status and goes toward defining the latter as well. It encompasses all the actions expected to be carried out within the configuration of rights and obligations of a status or structured position a person occupies within a group. It includes the way he or she defines himself or herself and the behaviour appropriate to his or her position and also the way others define him or her and the behaviour they expect from him or her.[3]

Thus, individual role can be related to three aspects: the individual's own ideas about what is appropriate (role cognition); other people's ideas about what is appropriate (role expectation) and other people's ideas about what he or she should do (norms).[4]

Role consists of "the expectations that persons hold in common towards any person who falls in a particular category by virtue of his position in the social system".[5] It is a "behaviour that is characterized and expected of a person or persons who occupy a position in the group".[6] It is an internally consistent series of conditioned responses by one member of a serial situation which represents the stimulus for a similarly, internally consistent series of conditioned responses of the other in a serial situation.[7] Sargent writes that a person's role is a pattern or type of social behaviour which seems situationally appropriate to him in terms of the demands and expectations of those in his group.[8]

Biddle and Thomas have pointed out that the most common definition of role is as a set of prescriptions that define the desired behaviour of a position occupant. In other words role is regularities in one person's behavioural relationship to another and these regularities are governed by norms or shared acceptance of the same rules prescribing appropriate behaviour.[9] According to Biddle and Thomas, five terms are relevant in understanding role-related behaviour: expectation, norms, performance, evaluation and sanction.[10]

Clarity of definitions of role is reduced, firstly by discrepancies between what is given verbally and what is demonstrated in 'practice', and secondly by the inconsistency in the response to and expectation from the actor on the part of other individuals in the counter positions. Thirdly, where a society assigns or permits more than one role to a particular position, the degree of adjustment of the incumbent to the role varies with the compatibility of the roles. Finally, when incompatible roles belong to a given category of roles, the degree of adjustment varies directly with the extent to which techniques for resolving or minimizing conflicts are available.[11]

Role Conflict

In certain situations role conflict occurs. That is, the situations are so structured that an actor is required to fill simultaneously two or more roles that present contradictory or even mutually exclusive expectations. The actor cannot realistically conform to these expectations. This usually happens when a woman has to perform the roles of a housewife and an employee. Simultaneously, due to different personality dispositions and personal characteristics, role conflict may be accentuated. In other words, the attributes of the actor may be to determine the degree of felt conflict.[12] The term 'role strain'[13] or 'role stress'[14] which represents a particular emphasis, has been used, but the central component of all of the formulations is 'incompatibility'. Thus, role conflict, role strain or role stress are all concerned with problems for the individual which arise as a result of role incompatibilities.[15] Role conflict studies adopt various approaches to the examination of role incompatibilities. Seeman's analysis of the school superintendent's role focussed on "situation in which the observer notes what appears to be conflicting sets of expectations".[16] Other studies involve either of the two main categories: perceptual ones attempt to measure the role occupant's perception of conflicting expectations or orientations. It is clear that while a social situation may be one which to the observer is charged with conflict, the role occupants may or may not perceive this.[17] Perceptual experimental studies attempt to measure the degree of effective concern over incompatibilities and relate those to certain characteristics of the role occupant, including personality variables.[18]

Working Women and Role Conflict

Working women, especially married working women have to play a dual role: one, rooted in the family as daughter (or daughter-in-law), wife, mother and housewife, and the other as employee. Being subjected to the dual demands of home and work, they are liable to face a crisis of adjustment. In addition to the biological function, which they have to perform because of their sex, and culturally defined woman's roles, they are confronted with responsibilities, and duties connected with their employment. It is felt that working women are generally not very clear about the judicious performance of their dual roles. The changed context is considered to have created a role confusion for working women: to the established traditional roles, a new role of working outside the home and earning a salary has been added. The confusion arises due to inability on the part of a woman to strike all by herself a balance between the old roles and the new role. It could be made possible by redefining of the roles of the family members in terms of duties and responsibilities. And, if the role and expectation of the family members of working women do not change or get redefined in terms of duties and responsibilities, there are greater chances of conflicts.[19] The role conflict to which generally the Indian working women are exposed due to entry into jobs are above all 'inter-role conflict'.[20]

Yogendra Singh remarks: "The ensuing role conflict of working women who have heavy responsibilities both in the household and the office has been a subject of inquiry. The role conflict of women as mother, wife, employee, etc., demands of them not only additional resourcefulness in values, emotions and role-commitments but also wider institutional support from society. It tends deeply to affect the self-image that women have of themselves, and some studies show it to be a material element in their being able to move towards social, economic, cultural and political equality. Gorwaney found self-image to be an important subjective element in the value profile of women students. It contributed to their objective search for social equality (Gorwaney, 1977). Other studies have analysed aspects of role conflict among women in different domains of responsibilities (Chakraborthy, 1978; Kapur, 1970; Jha, 1985; Khanna et al., 1978; Mehta, 1975).[21]

Adjustment

Adjustment is a process, which is expected to lead to a happy and contended life of a person. It creates a balance between needs and the capacity to meet these needs, persuades the persons involved to change ways of life according to the demands of the situation, and gives strength and ability to bring desirable changes in the conditions of the environment.

Working women have to adjust themselves at home as well as work place. For them, adjustment is "smooth switch over from one status to other status, perceiving roles as perceived by others, and performing multiple roles with efficiency and satisfaction".

The requirement to be self-sacrificing for the fulfilment of their subordinate gender role arises because of the demands of marriage and career.[22]

'Adjustment' is used to refer to a situation in which a woman is required to adjust herself to a situation which is new or indifferent to her. Thus, if her parents do not allow her to work, she adjusts, if she goes to live with orthodox in-laws, she adjusts to their ways. In doing so, a woman adopts rationalizations which help her to accept her fate. Adjustment also takes the form of a highly developed sensitivity towards the needs and wishes of others. The most artful women become master-mind in manipulating others impressions about themselves. They learn to wait for the proper time, circumstances and issues on which they can express their own point of view. As soon as married, the young bride is expected to look up to her husband as lord and master, anticipate his 'will and wish', and cater to his needs and her obligations to her in laws. Her socialization has taught her the art of bowing before elders. In effect, she practices the same art of adjustment that she learned.[23]

Performance of Multiple Roles

Employed women face the problem of adjustment because of their varied role expectations. They are required to perform multiple and at times conflicting roles. A woman is expected to the perform roles of a homemaker, wife, mother, employee, etc. at the same time. Being simultaneously confronted with the multiple demands of home and outside, women have to face the problem of adjustment.

Difficulty arises often because divergent and conflicting roles make demands on women without taking into consideration their physical capacity, energy, endurance and time, which are certainly finite.

Since the role expectations are poles apart, a sort of conflict arises normally between an employed woman and her husband and in-laws. Theoretically speaking, such a problem could not arise if employment and home were considered as two mutually exclusive fields of life. With the erosion of the traditional ideas, the problem of adjustment of working women becomes more serious. A typical woman is dedicated to her family additionally, by earning money. But, due to this diverse role expectation, she often wonders whether the additional money which she earns by working is worth the sacrifice she is making by taking up the job. Hence, a job is considered, at times, as a hurdle by working women.[24]

The focus is on multiple roles creating the feelings of guilt, anxiety, strain and tension among working women. For this purpose, only married working women were selected for the study of performance of multiple roles because it was expected that the married women who have family responsibilities have more adjustment problems than unmarried ones.

There is difference in the perception of performance of multiple roles among the women. They belong to different class categories and have experience of both role conflict and the role congruency. A total of 68.3 percent of them performed their roles satisfactorily as compared to 35.6 percent who were not satisfied with their performance of the dual role and had a feeling of role conflict. Likewise, 80 percent of women of category one and category two have experienced the highest degree of role congruency, whereas role dissatisfaction is highest among 40 percent of category three. Category five consists of the business class and only 25 percent women of this category are working satisfactorily.

The women belonging to category one, are overconscious of their duties and obligations towards parents, husbands and children and they have not been able to do justice to their family and the household duties. This creates a problem of inner conflict and tension which they experience, particularly if they are very keen to run both, their homes and career extremely efficiently and are desirous of paying equal attention to their home and work.

Reason for Work and Adjustment Pattern

The highest percentage of women was working mainly due to gross economic necessity or to supplement the husband's insufficient income or to raise the standard of living. The rest have cited other factors as their primary reason for working.

For the analysis of reason and adjustment patterns, the subjects are arranged into two groups—one group consists of those women who are working primarily for economic need, to help their families; in these cases their own satisfaction is not the primary reason. The other group consists of those women who are working for non-economic reasons, for some kind of personal satisfaction—emotional, intellectual or social and to whom financial gain is only secondary.

The majority of the women of category one and category two work for non-economic reasons whereas 88 percent of women of category three and 95 percent of women of category four work for economic reasons. Similarly, the extent of dissatisfaction is also greater among women of category three and category four as compared to 20 percent of women of category one and two respectively. It is significant that 90 percent of women of category five work for economic reasons and 75 percent among them are dissatisfied.

The economic reason is one of the primary reasons among the majority of women going for work. The higher the economic status the lower is the number of women going for work for economic reasons and the lower the economic status, the higher is the number of women going to work for economic reasons. Thus, the higher the economic status, lower is the degree of role-conflict, and the lower the economic status, the higher is the extent of role conflict. Women who go out to work for non-economic reasons, work not due to any compulsion but for their personal satisfaction. On the other hand, women working for their economic needs are compelled to work by the circumstances, or by the needs of others. Thus, the extent of adjustment is positively related to the primary reason for work.

Occupational Status and Role-Conflict between Spouses

Working women are facing the problem of their identity. When women perform duties of a specific nature involving decision-making and discretion to exercise authority as working women, they need to be identified as independent role performers. But as wives and mothers they are made to comply with the husband's words and also to follow the directives of in-laws. Such a situation inevitably correlates role-ambiguity and role-conflict. Just as they would normally not desire to impose their personal whims and fancies over their official subordinates, they would not like to submit to authoritarian decisions and impositions of husbands and in-laws. An imbalance of this equation normally creates marital discord. Ignoring the primacy of obligations affects adversely the domestic and marital happiness, hence the maladjustment. "The issue, therefore, is not one of the superiority and independence of spouse; it is primarily a matter of mutual adjustment and maintenance of harmony."[25] Marital harmony of the working women depends on several factors like the husband's acceptance of his wife's participation in economic life. If the husband does not like it, then the domestic harmony is disturbed. Several studies have shown that there may be husbands who may like the economic participation of the wife but not its consequences in the form of her neglect of domestic duties and responsibilities. It is important to know whether employment of women has led to marital adjustment or maladjustment.

About 82 percent of the women of category one and 55 percent of the women of category two replied in the negative, i.e., that they have no role conflict with their husbands. Similarly, 56 percent of the women of category three and 70 percent of the women of category four and 65 percent of the women of category five (women in business) also replied in the negative. According to the majority of the women, marital harmony is a matter of mutual adjustment and reciprocity of relations. There were also 31.6 percent of the total number of women who experienced role conflict due to their job.

When a woman is an 'earning wife', she expects from her husband likewise employed, an equal amount of domestic work or the appointment of servants. When, in the face of these demands, the husband or in-laws insist that domestic work is the exclusive duty of the wife, tensions cannot be avoided.[26] A total of 31.6 percent of the women suffered this type of conflict. Here the demand of a wife that the husband should help is a direct attack on his 'privileged' husband status; for, to serve the husband gladly and without hesitation is the highest duty of a good Hindu wife. Since the majority of the husbands are still not ready to accept this changing reality, it results in a state of role-conflict.[27]

Neglect of Children

Children always need the loving attention, care and protection of both parents. They are particularly dependent on the affection and attention provided by their mother. The effect of the mother's employment on the mother-child relationship depends on a variety of factors: her capacity for providing a good substitute or arrangement for child the during her absence, the cooperation she receives from family members, ages of the children, etc.

A minor child may never like the working of his mother whereas a grown-up child possesses both a favourable as well as an unfavourable disposition towards the mother's working. The capacity of a working mother to offer additional gift items or other demands made by her children may make them appreciate her working, even if any inconvenience is faced by them at the time of her working outside. During the absence of a working mother, a child has to take care of himself or do home work all alone. "Children are not mature enough to judge whether their mother's working is good or bad. In general they do feel proud of their working mother's achievements".[28]

The study reveals that 85.4 percent of working women are fully satisfied with their child care arrangement. In contrast to these women who are well adjusted, 24.5 percent are those who suffer from a feeling of guilt. There is no definite relationship between the feeling of guilt and occupational status as the percentage of women of upper class suffering from this feeling of guilt is almost the same as that of the women belonging to the lower class.

Family and Role Conflict

The composition or pattern of family also influences adjustment of working mothers in a nuclear family. Working women have to make adjustments with their husbands and children, who are expected to be cooperative and considerate. In extended families, the wife is to live and adjust with her husband's relatives who may not be so cooperative and considerate. Thus, persons living in nuclear families are likely to be more adjusted and happy than the persons living in joint families.[29]

Majority of working women, i.e., 80 percent, living in joint families experience role conflict as compared to 20 percent of women living in nuclear families. Most of those living in nuclear families wanted more independence and hence they did not relish having the in-laws with them. The majority of women living in joint families become narrow in their outlook and view the joint family as a source of conflict for them.

Performance of Job Roles and Job Commitment

Performance of job roles depends upon several conditions. It is expected that higher the occupation, higher the income and favourable working conditions, etc., will affect the role satisfaction of the employee of any organization and will help in adjustment better than in the case of those working at lower levels. A total of 76.7 percent of women belonging to various class categories are highly satisfied with their role performance at work.

In all, 60 percent of the women of category one are found to be highly committed to their work, as compared to 90 percent of the women of category four. It is noticeable that husband's attitude is very significant in this matter. The husband's positive approach in spite of non-sharing of household chores, considerably satisfies working women.

Behaviour Patterns

The behaviour of officers at work place is very important for the working women. The study indicates that 65.8 percent women feel that the officers behave sympathetically, 23.2 percent of women feel that the behaviour of officers is casual whereas 10.9 percent complained about the contemptuous behaviour patterns of the officers towards them.

Molestation

We often hear too, of frightful and shocking incidents of molestation of women employees at work. Officers were involved in molesting women employees at the work place. So, it was necessary to know from the women about this type of behaviour of officers.

Only 2.5 percent of women became the victim of molestation by officer at work. It is noticeable that not even a single woman became the victim of molestation by officers in the category of one and two at work. Even though, the number of women who were molested is very small yet, this indicates that the reports about molestation of women employees are not baseless.

Attitude

The study of role perception and attitudes of women is most relevant in the context of modernization as well as the status of women in the society. Attitude is a kind of mental mechanism, which is used by people when their psychological equilibrium is threatened by any activity of another person.[30] According to Rammers,[31] the attitude of a person or a group of persons has a far-reaching effect on their overt and covert behaviour, for attitudes are theoretically a component of all behaviour, both overt and covert. Since the attitude of a person is central to his subjective life and largely determines his thoughts, feelings, and behaviour, it is very significant to know the attitudes of a person and more so, the changes taking place in their attitudes, if one wants to study the change or the direction towards which society is moving.

A woman or working woman has to take care of the responsibilities related to her job in addition to her household duties. The latter are linked to her role and status in the family. Therefore, 'attitude' of a woman or working woman towards her work is influenced by several factors governed by her family background and/or social life or her mental perception of all these. On the other hand, the 'attitude towards' a woman or working woman reflects in a major way the family and socio-cultural configuration of the society she belongs to, which influences her life. But, the 'attitudes of' and 'attitudes towards' are in no way unidirectional parallel lines of interactions. Similarly, the 'attitudes towards' a working woman can lead the woman to assume a disposition which in turn has a bearing on her family and/or the society. In short, the recurring patterns of attitudinal reactions and behaviour of any one can, to a significant extent, be traced through the analysis of their socio-cultural background and they have the potential to bring about change in the socio-cultural fabric itself.[32]

It is expected that change in the perception and attitudes would lead to the acceptance of modern values which point to the equality of men and women. The traditional value system of society supported subordination and dependence on the part of women in their relations with men. But modern values point towards equality of status for women.

Attitude Towards Nuclear Family

The majority of the women in the study (81%) favoured the nuclear family whereas 19 percent had a negative attitude towards the nuclear family. In fact, in a joint family, a woman living with in-laws does not enjoy freedom and she is required to carry out the instructions of her elder and even younger in-laws. Employed women find the general atmosphere in a joint family intolerable. It is noticeable that 81 percent of the women expressed their disliking for the joint family as it created difficulties in the proper socialization of their children.

Attitude Towards Marriage

Traditionally, marriages are arranged by parents in our society. But, in the last few years, there seems to have been a trend in favour of self-arranged marriages. So, it is very important to know the attitudes of women towards the types of marriages. The majority of the women in the study (75%) have favoured arranged marriages whereas 25 percent of women have favoured love marriages or self-arranged marriages. In fact, the majority of those who favoured arranged marriages, belonged to lower economic and educational status. It is significant that 25 percent of the women with higher education and higher occupational statuses were not in favour of tradition-oriented arranged marriages.

Attitude towards Job and Domestic Responsibilities

The study reveals that 30.5 percent of the women in the study are of the view that for a woman both roles are equally important, whereas 37 percent of the women are of the view that the domestic role is more important for a woman and 32.5 percent of the women are of the opinion that job role is more important for the progress and career of a woman.

The study also shows that 70 percent of the women are of the opinion that a working woman can perform both roles satisfactorily whereas 30 percent of the women felt that a working woman cannot do justice to either of her roles—her domestic role and her professional role.

Attitude Towards Socialization of Children

It is important to know women's attitude towards traditional sex roles—whether boys should also be trained like girls to look after the home. It is significant that 90 percent of the women are in favour of equal socialization of their sons and daughters whereas only 10 percent of the women were of the view that boys and girls should not be trained similarly because of their basic biological and social roles.

Attitude Towards Equality of Status

It is significant to know how far the notion of equality (equal status with men in real life) is found among the highly educated women. Nearly 14 percent of the women are of the view that they enjoy equality with men, whereas 86 percent of the women accept that it does not exist in reality.

Attitude Towards Superiority of Men

In our society, male sex is still treated as superior. But, with educational and employment opportunities, it was expected that there would be a change in the traditional thinking. Thus, it is significant to know what women felt about the notion of the 'superiority of man'. While 75 percent of the women still believe in the superiority of men over women, 25 percent of the women did not believe in the superiority of men over women.

Thus, it is significant that there is role conflict but there is positive relationship between reason of work and pattern of adjustment. The question is only of higher level or lower level of adjustment. It is also significant that the attitude and role of the husband is quite important in the emancipation of women.

Notes

1. Yogendra Singh, *Essays on Modernization in India*, Manohar, New Delhi, 1978, pp. 76-77.
2. Ibid., p. 77.
3. T.M. Newcomb, *Social Psychology*, The Dryden Press, New York, 1950.

   J.T. Gullahorn, "Measuring Role Conflict", *American Journal of Sociology*, 1956, pp. 209-303.

   Sarita Sahay, *Tribal Women in the New Profile*, Anmol Publications Pvt. Ltd., 2002, pp. 80-81.
4. Michael R. Banton, *An Introduction to the Study of Social Relations*, Tavistock Publications, London, 1968.
5. P.F. Sacord and C.W. Backman, *Social Psychology*, McGraw Hill, New York, 1964, p. 457.
6. E.E. Jones and H.B. Geard, *Foundation of Social Psychology*, New York: Wiley, 1967, p. 718.
7. Jr. L.S. Cottrell, "The Adjustment of the Individual to his Age and Sex Roles", *American Sociological Review*, 4, 1942, pp. 617-20.
8. S.S. Sargent, "Conception of Role and Ego in Contemporary Psychology", in J. Rohrer and Sherif (ed.), *Social Psychology at Crossroads*, New York: Harper, 1951.
9. B.J. Biddle and E.J. Thomas, *Role Theory: Concept and Research*, (ed.), New York: Wiley, 1966.

   Also see, T.M. Newcomb, Turner and P.E. Converse, *Social Psychology*, New York: Holt, Reinhart and Winston, 1965.
10. B.J. Biddle and E.J. Thomas, op. cit.
11. Rita Sood, *Changing Status and Adjustment of Women*, Manak Publications Pvt. Ltd., Delhi, Jaipur, 1991, p. 94.
12. Pushpa Sinha, *Role Conflict Among the Working Women*, Janki Prakashan, Patna, 1986.
13. G.J. Goode, "A Theory of Role Strain", *American Sociological Review*, Vol. 25(4), pp. 483-96.
14. L.J. Westwood, "The Role of the Teacher", *Educational Research*, IX(2), 1967a, pp. 122-34.
15. G.R. Grace, *Ròle Conflict and Teacher*, London: Routledge and Kegan Paul, 1972, p. 2.
16. M. Seeman, "Role Conflict and Ambivalence in Leadership", *American Sociological Review*, 18, p. 373.

17. L.J. Westwood, op. cit.
18. J.W. Getzels and E.G. Guba, "Role, Role Conflict and Effectiveness", *American Sociological Review*, 19, 1954, pp. 164-75.
19. Sarita Sahay, op. cit., p. 82.
20. M. Mies, *Indian Women and Patriarchy*, Concept Publications, New Delhi, 1980.
21. Yogendra Singh, *Indian Sociology: Social Conditioning and Emerging Concerns*, Vistaar Publications, New Delhi, 1986, p. 91.
22. Sarita Sahay, op. cit., pp. 90-91.
23. Rita Sood, op. cit., p. 92.
24. Ibid., pp. 95-96.
25. Ibid., p. 100.
26. Ibid., p. 102.
27. Ibid., p. 102.
28. Sarita Sahay, op. cit., pp. 72-73.
29. Rita Sood, op. cit., p. 104.
30. S.K. Mangal, 1984, *Abnormal Psychology*, Sterling Publishers Pvt. Ltd., New Delhi.
31. H.H. Rammers, *Introduction to Opinion and Attitude Measurement*, New York: Harper and Brothers, 1954, p. 3.
32. Sarita Sahay, op. cit., p. 41.

References

Chakraborthy, Krishna, *The Conflicting Worlds of Working Mothers*, Progressive Publishers, Culcutta, 1978.

Gorwaney, N., *Self Image and Social Change: A Study of Female Students*, Sterling Publishers, New Delhi, 1977.

Jha, K.N., *Women Towards Modernization*, Janki Prakashan, Patna, 1985.

Kapur, P., *Marriage and the Working Women in India*, Vikas, Delhi, 1970.

Khanna, G. et al., *Indian Women Today*, Vikas, New Delhi, 1978.

Mehta, R., *Divorced Hindu Women*, Vikas, New Delhi, 1975.

Sarbin, Theodore R., "Role Theory", in *Handbook of Social Psychology*, Vol. 1, (ed.), Gardner Lindsey, Addison-Wesley, London, 1954.

6

Aspirations and Values

Yogendra Singh writes: "The modernization of role structures involves changes not only in norms and behaviour but also in the psychic-dynamic properties, bringing about major changes in the motivational and value orientation patterns of individuals. Motivationally, modernized role structures represent a higher level of psychic mobility and achievement orientation; the latter stimulates the aspiration levels generally in a modern society. Thus, modernization also implies a revolution in aspiration levels. Aspiration may broadly be defined as the strength of an individual's motivation to achieve progressively higher (or, conversely, lower) goals based on the experiences of success and failure, his own and of others who constitute his reference models. [Aspiration level may be 'higher' or 'lower' in a temporal sense (between two points of time) for the same individual, or it may be 'higher' or 'lower' in comparison to that of some other individuals. In the former case aspiration operates as a psychological category, but in the latter situation it has both psychological as well as socio-cultural foundations].

Traditional Indian society was hierarchical, its stratification was closed. Communication was segmental and localised, and social mobility occurred under only exceptional circumstances. All these served to circumscribe individual motivations, culturally as well as existentially, and individual aspirations were correspondingly stabilized.

During modernization, these traditional structures and institutions change adaptively—in response to new demands—without total self-transformation; and many new institutions also emerge. Societal segments show a new energy for wider interaction and integration; exclusive segments like caste and ethnic group seek equality in social participation and in the sharing of resources, pressing for egalitarian norms in disguised form, without renouncing the principles of exclusiveness or inequality. Such 'democratic incarnations' of traditional structures generate radically new motivational and evaluative perspective whose consequences are revolutionary. Individualism is ushered in without alienation. Aspirations seek a new high level, without hedonistic voluntarism in behaviour fully replacing the traditional moral voluntarism. The consequences of the revolution of aspirations which pervade the society depend on the latter's capacity to absorb the psychological and social tensions so energised. When effectively canalised, the aspirations generated in a modern role structure can make for continual innovation and adaptive changes."[1]

The major source of the individual's aspirations and goals is the values and norms of his reference groups. These norms and values enter as a frame of reference and affect the goals and aspirations. The various reference groups, which influence the aspirations of the individual, are: family, school, college, play group, friend circle and other social and cultural groups. Of all the social groups that influence the growth of personality and ultimately the aspirations, the most important is undoubtedly the family.[2]

In Indian society, at present, both traditional values (inequalitarian) and modern values (equalitarian) exist as Srinivas has also commented.[3] During the last two decades, emergence of new values has clearly been seen and experienced. An adult mother of the present, since she herself has suffered due to inequalitarian values, does not want her daughters to become their victims, but at the same time she is not able to pick up the courage to protest completely against the social system and traditions. At the same time, girls from modern families are seen protesting against this discrimination and to some extent are able to get rid of it also.

Working women, as Chatterjee has said, are wandering in the market like blind people, seeking their own identity, through their personal work, without leaving their traditional role.[4] In the name of compromise with circumstances in the professional field they accept whatever they get easily and for whatever they do not get, they prepare themselves mentally, use some defence mechanism and do not become much upset. At the home front also they become used to annoyance and complaints of family members. In this way, married working women, have to struggle very hard from the physical, mental and social points of view. Husbands of this class expect too much from their wives. They want them to perform all types of roles, e.g., traditional and modern, inside and outside home.

For unmarried women it is a very big problem as to how she should work and behave with men, colleagues, friends, senior officials, etc. They have to protect their cultural background and ideals and at the same time they have to become partners in interactions and interrelations with their colleagues also. As Vohra and Sen have expressed, as long as unmarried girls work, their parents continue to face difficulties regarding their marriages. Due to high ambitions regarding the potential husband they keep on rejecting normal proposals. As they keep on climbing the stairs of success in their profession on the one hand, their marriage gets more and more delayed, on the other. A time comes when in the absence of a good proposal they have to either marry an unwanted man or remain unmarried.

Non-working women have no status of their own in society. They enjoy more or less status according to their father's or husband's status. The biggest problem of non-working women is their lower status in the family due to economic dependence.[5]

They are struggling for the new identity. Hence, it is very significant to know whether the changes in the socio-cultural structure have promoted high aspirations, and values amongst the highly educated women or the changes have further created tensions and more conflicts amongst them.

Educational Aspirations

Education as an activity requires a definite investment of time, energy and resources. Even if education was made wholly free, people may still be unwilling to take it because the expenditure of energy and time that this pursuit may require may still mean a loss of resources which one would create if one were to go in for some other activity during the same time. Therefore, the question whether they are ultimately ready or willing to make the necessary investment of time, energy and resources in education is likely to be dependent upon whether they see this investment as commensurate with what education can give or gives them in return. If they feel that returns from education are not going to be commensurate with whatever their perception of their lifestyles are, they are unlikely to go in for or send children for education, no matter how attractive a proposition it might be from the viewpoint of spread of modern outlook and modernization. On the contrary, if they find that the returns from it are likely to be commensurate with their future hopes and aspirations, they will not only be willing but will indeed go out of their way to make sacrifices for the sake of education.[6]

The study reveals that 60 percent of the women have aspirations for higher degrees, whereas 20 percent have aspirations for higher research for better career and status in the job. 20 percent of the women are unable to express their educational aspirations.

As regards the educational aspirations for their children, 83.5 percent of the women are with the aspirations of technical/ medical degrees for their children. About 10 percent of the women are with the aspirations of non-technical higher degrees and 5 percent of the women aspire for commerce degrees for their children. The study reveals that the women are with the educational aspirations for their children from the occupational point of view. Only 1.5 percent women are unable to express the educational aspirations they have for their children.

Occupational Aspirations

The aspiration for profession or occupation was limited to one's own stratum. The young generally accepted this pattern, but the ascription of occupations on the basis of one's membership of a particular group does not exist today, at least in theory.[7] Now occupational ascription has been replaced by individual occupational selection which is done on the basis of one's personal achievements through education, training and experience.

In examining the occupational aspirations of highly educated women, we have tried to analyse the occupational mobility and the traditional pattern of occupation (e.g., in terms of their father's pattern of education) along with their present state of occupation and occupational aspirations for their children.

There is a significant difference in the professional aspirations of the women for their children in comparison to their own professional standing. There is some difference between their father's/husband's occupational status. Only in the categories of farming and traditional occupations, there is not even a single woman who has these aspirations for her children. The women are not engaged in farming or traditional occupations categories. In the category of business, only 12.9 percent of the women in the study are engaged in business in comparison to 32.2 percent of their fathers/husbands. But only 6.4 percent of women of this category have aspirations for business for their children.

In this study, 77.5 percent of the women are included in this aspect because 22.5 percent of women are engaged only in household affairs as they are housewives or they are studying in educational institutions. But, they have occupational aspirations for their children. While 90 percent amongst them have aspirations for technical/medical/administrative jobs, 8 percent have aspirations for government jobs, whereas only 2 percent have aspirations for business for their children.

Achievements

As regards the achievements of the children, 37.5 percent of women in the study are those having children who are settled, whereas 35 percent of the women had minor children, 15 percent of the women are married but did not have any issue as yet and 12.5 percent of the women are still unmarried. Hence, 7.5 percent of the women's children are in technical/medical/administrative jobs, 28.5 percent of the women's children are in general service and 1.5 percent of the women's children are engaged in business.

Satisfaction

An individual cannot remain satisfied with high aspirations and achievements if his/her aspiration level is high. Thus the degree of satisfaction and aspiration level is inversely co-related. 20 percent of the women are highly satisfied and 80 percent are less satisfied with their high aspirations for their status and occupation and also occupational aspirations for their children. Whereas 84 percent of the women are highly satisfied and 16 percent of women are less satisfied with their low aspirations for their occupation as well as occupational aspirations for their children.

Values

Parsons regarded value as a normative pattern which defined desirable behaviour for a system in relation to its environment, without differentiation in terms of the functions of units or of their particular situations.[8] As values are cultural products they differ from culture to culture and from time to time. Values in relation to tradition and modernity have been analysed very scientifically by Yogendra Singh.

Yogendra Singh writes: "Cultural values have a pattern and constitute a system which is embedded in a society's history and mythology. This historical-mythical character of cultural values gives them an inherent dynamism as well as stability. Whether a particular cultural system is change-prone or impervious to change depends upon the historicity of social processes. Cultural systems, nevertheless, have some universal attributes which transcend the historicity of traditions. One such attribute is, differentiation in all cultural systems between those values which are of instrumental significance and those which are of an intrinsic or fundamental significance and those which are of an intrinsic or fundamental concern. The former are values which serve as means to an end, and the latter comprise an end in themselves. The fundamental values of society constitute its core values and govern the adaptive power and direction of the instrumental cultural values and its other manifestations."[9]

Analysing traditional Indian culture, Yogendra Singh writes: "Traditionally, the dominant themes of cultural values in India were characterized by *hierarchy, holism, continuity* and *transcendence*".[10] Of these, "the hierarchy-value constituted the core of the value system."[11]

"Similarly, it would be erroneous to say that the traditional Indian cultural system was static. On the contrary, it did experience several movements for change. Such movements took place from within the framework of the traditional culture, mostly through internal growth and most such processes of change led primarily to deviant adaptations within the traditional frame, rather than to revolutionary cultural alternatives. The symbolic universe of these deviant cultural movements remained more or less confined within the realm of the cultural values of *hierarchy, holism, continuity* and *transcendence*. Buddhism, Jainism, Bhakti movements and the cultural tradition of Islam and Christianity, could all be treated as adaptive rather than revolutionary, forms of cultural movements."[12]

About the contemporary challenges to Indian cultural values, Singh writes: "The contemporary challenge to Indian cultural values has its basis in historicity. According to a view, the very phenomenon of contemporaneity poses a serious challenge to tradition. The proponents of this viewpoint hold that tradition by its nature can reflect not historicity but only continuity, and the notion of contemporaneity introduces a schism in the structure of tradition, rendering its conception problematic. This problematics is rooted into the enigmatic character of the relationship between tradition and temporality, the two being antithetical to each other. Thus, contemporaneity as an attribute of tradition cannot be treated without creating logical obsolescence of the very notion of tradition. Obviously, this conception of tradition is primarily aprioristic and metaphysical and it does not posit any existential or sociological merit in the character of tradition. To this school of thought, tradition is an abstract configuration of revealed principles rather than a socio-historical reality.

Obviously, a sociological conceptualization of tradition is contradistinct from the above viewpoint. Nevertheless, this viewpoint highlights how fundamental is the schism that contemporaneity or historicity introduces in the traditional definition of cultural values. This also adds significance to the fundamental issues implicit in contemporary challenges to Indian cultural values.

The first question that arises in the assessment of the nature of contemporary challenges to the traditional cultural values is that of formulation of the nature of these challenges. These challenges have their historical bases in the colonialism of our society. Colonialism not only meant the economic and political subordination of Indian society to an alien society but also an encounter of our cultural system to a worldview fundamentally discrepant in nature and fraught with contradictions. It heralded an encounter of the Indian traditional values of *hierarchy, holism, continuity* and *transcendence* with a system of values and worldview which was sharply in contrast and which had emerged through a process of a longdrawn revolutionary transformation of society, the breakdown of the medieval social structure and the onset of the industrial revolution.

This encounter of India with the west had indeed both cultural and structural ramifications which have led to the evolution of contemporary challenges in our cultural values. The western contact meant a revolutionary change in the traditional values. It implied introjection of the value of equality in place of *hierarchy*, of *individualism* as replacement of *holism*, of *historicity* in place of *continuity* and of *techno-scientific rationalism* in place of the principle of *transcendence*. In ideal-typical sense, for the new values to get institutionalized it was indeed required of the Indian social and cultural system too to undergo a fundamental and revolutionary transformation.

Sociologically, the opposition that we have postulated between the traditional values of *hierarchy, holism, continuity* and *transcendence* and the western values of equality, individualism, historicity and techno-scientific rationalism have a purely heuristic relevance. Yet, this scheme offers a possibility for analytical treatment of the empirical nature of the response that Indian culture and society have made to the Western challenges, and the self-transformation that the Indian culture has undergone in this process.

Heuristically, the cultural value of equality also implies transition from the principle of status and structural closure to that of classes, professions and extended open forms of social differentiation. Similarly, *individualism* inheres with it the supplementary values of performance orientation instead of quality ascription we find in the value of *holism*. *Historicity* in contradistinction to the value system of *continuity* would imply emphasis on temporality, rational time-budgeting and above all deeper commitment to the belief that human beings by their own efforts could change their life-situations. Unlike the value of *continuity* which is devoid of time-consciousness, *historicity* has time-commitment as its major value frame. Finally, rationality and secularism in the western cultural model imply a scientific-technological worldview which is essentially materialistic and probabilistic and is opposed to the principle of *transcendence* of the traditional culture.

This contradistinction between the traditional cultural values of India and the modern values historically framed in a colonial background marks the onset of the challenges to our cultural system. These challenges could be noticed both at the cultural as well as social structural levels."[13]

Hierarchy and Equality

According to Yogendra Singh, "the principle of hierarchy systematically represented the worldview of traditional Indian culture. It permeated the domains of normative structure, conception of human nature, principles of institutionalization of social actions and cosmology. Hierarchy implied a relationship between the fundamental and instrumental values of the Indian society in which the former governed the latter. Logically, other than values of hierarchy, no institution of our society had autonomy in its functions, be it the economic or familial or political institution. Hierarchy in a manner encompassed all other social and cultural principles.

Other secondary attributes of hierarchy were: the pre-eminence of sacred over pragmatic values, emphasis on status rather than class in social stratification, and emphasis on vocation rather than occupation in economic life."[14]

There are three main types of equality: (1) *Equality of opportunity*: The provision of equality of access to institutions and social positions among relevant social groups, such as equality of entry to university for students of both sexes, and all class origins. (2) *Equality of condition*: Equality in the conditions of life for all relevant social groups, such as equality of incomes. It is impossible to maximize equality of opportunity without attending also to equality of condition. Proponents of equality of opportunity who relish the differential benefits obtained by persons of different abilities ignore the material and cultural advantages which one generation of the successful is able to transmit to the next. Inequalities of condition obstruct equality of opportunity; all do not start from the same point. (3) *Equality of result or outcome*: The application of different policies or processes to different social groups in order to transform inequalities at the beginning into equalities at the end. Positive discrimination in favour of women or blacks or the inner city poor in educational and occupational selection, for example, is meant to compensate for inequalities of condition which would otherwise make nonsense of equality of opportunity.

Social equality is not synonymous with classlessness. Definitions of class vary, but they all allow that the elimination of class does not of itself remove all social inequalities.[15]

Holism and Individualism

According to Yogendra Singh, "holism implied pre-eminence of collective interests over the individual. It formed a secondary attribute of hierarchy since the values of universalistic-collectivism logically harmonised with and reinforced the principle of hierarchy".[16] Singh further writes: "Similarly holism implied commitment to the value of universalistic-collectivism as against universalistic individualism which forms the ethos of liberal social ideology. By itself holism as values comes close to the Marxist notion of socialism or communism but being a part of the *package* of the principle of hierarchy which not only rejects class for status (caste) but also embodies the value of continuity based on the faith in the theory of rebirth and cyclical view of time it contradicts the worldview."[17]

Individualism—an approach to normative political theorizing that assigns significance solely to the interest and/or freedom of individual persons, and treats these as the only criteria for defining the conditions of justice, political obligations and the satisfaction of the public interest. Individualistic political theories srepudiate accounts of these conditions that refer to the circumstances of collectivities (e.g., classes, nations, races, the human species) and are not reducible to statements about the circumstances of persons. Though historically associated with 'liberalism' (see also natural rights), such theories bear only a contingent connection to it (see Hobbes; Utilitarianism). They specify the proper scope of 'state' activity—which may be minimal or extensive—in terms of what is required to secure the 'liberty' or maximum well-being of individuals.[18]

Continuity and Historicity

The value of continuity is based on faith in the theory of rebirth and cyclical view of time. Yogendra Singh writes: "*Hierarchy* along with the values of *holism* and *continuity* would have rendered the traditional Indian cultural system static, closed and impervious to human interventions for changes."[19]

According to Yogendra Singh, "*historicity* in contradistinction to the value system of *continuity* would imply emphasis on temporality, rational time-budgeting and above all deeper commitment to the belief that human beings by their own efforts could change their life-situations. Unlike the value of *continuity* which is devoid of time consciousness, *historicity* has time commitment as its major value frame".[20]

Transcendence and Techno-Scientific Rationalism

Yogendra Singh writes: "The principle of *transcendence* represents the values of human initiative in the traditional Indian culture. This principle ensured some degree of freedom to individuals for overcoming the constraints imposed by the hierarchical worldview of the traditional society. It had an existential as well as a metaphysical role to play in the traditional cultural system. Existentially, *transcendence* as a principle could be invoked by an individual to assert his individualism over the constraints both of *hierarchy* and *holism* in the cultural system."[21]

Rationalism—in a very general sense, an exaggerated belief in the 'rationality' of human beings, or the belief that all reality can in principle be understood by the human mind, that there are no ineluctable mysteries. Hence, a further sense of rationalism is the rejection of religion and superstition. In philosophy, the term has been applied to an 'epistemological' doctrine which, in opposition to 'empiricism', stresses the importance of deductive reasoning and a 'priori' theory in the creation of knowledge. Knowledge itself is seen as ideally forming a single, logically coherent system.[22]

As regards the analysis of values on the basis of responses, the women were classified into four categories of value holders: (i) pure traditional, (ii) traditional transitional, (iii) modern transitional, and (iv) pure modern.

Familism—Individualism

The study reveals that 1.5 percent of the women in the study are pure traditional, 60 percent of the women are traditional transitional, whereas 38.5 percent of women are modern transitional. It is very significant that not even a single woman is pure modern as far as these values are concerned.

Status and Class in Social Stratification

As regards the values of status, class in social stratification, 29 percent of women are traditional, 27.5 percent of women are traditional transitional and 58 percent of women are modern transitional, whereas not even a single woman in the study is in the category of pure modern. It is significant that 44.7 percent of women are modern transitional in the age group category of 31 to 40 years out of total 58 percent of women in the category of modern transitional.

Vocation and Occupation

As regards the vocation and occupation, 11.5 percent of women are traditional, 27 percent of women are traditional transitional and 61.5 percent of women are in the category of modern transitional. It is significant that not even a single woman among those studied is in the category of pure modern.

Conservatism and Progressivism

The term 'conservatism' is closely related to the term traditionalism. Ramsey et al defining conservatism state: "the value orientation towards traditionalism is an adoption of preçedence as the criteria in decision making and is the antithesis of social change." The term 'conservatism' appeared to be wider in scope as it was not restricted to decision making alone but produced an attitude which was favourable to the maintenance of 'status quo'. This *status quo* was the same as what Herskovits meant by "the phenomenon of cultural stability—a phenomenon which, in its psychological aspects, is called conservatism".[23]

Conservatism is a view about the desirable scope of policy and of constitutional change to any particular set of policies or institutions. It eschews policies which, to secure certain ends, aim to re-order large sectors of social life. It rejects fundamental alterations in existing institutions, holding that projects involving radical departures from prevailing arrangements fail to take account of human frailty, imperfect knowledge, and the inherently unmeasurable complexity of human affairs. This is attributed to an exaggerated 'rationalist' belief, on the part of radical reformers, in (1) the capacity of persons to allow general principles (rather than self-interest or unreflective prejudice) to govern their conduct; (2) the capacity of scientific thinking to generate models capable of capturing the multiformity of social life so as to yield reliable predictions for successful policy-design. The variety and uncertainty of human conduct are said to warrant only a pragmatic attitude to desirable political change, an attitude informed by the limits of the possible discovered through practice and example—rather—than theory—and thus vouchsafed to those whose experience of governing has imbued them with an appreciation of the time-tested and intricately interwoven traditions upon which the survival of a political community allegedly depends.[24]

Thus, conservatism is a positive attitude of the individual towards precedence and to the maintenance of status quo and hence unfavourable to the adoption of new ideas. Likewise, 'progressivism' is a positive attitude of the individual to change and to the adoption of new ideas. As regards these values, as observed in the study, 12.5 percent of women are traditional, 19 percent of women are traditional transitional and the majority, 68.5 percent of women are modern transitional in their approach. Significantly, no woman is pure modern in her approach.

Thus, education, occupation and age exert a considerable influence in determining the degrees of pure traditional, traditional transitional, modern transitional and pure modern values and approach of highly educated women.

Notes

1. Yogendra Singh, *Essays on Modernization*, Manohar, New Delhi, 1978, pp. 98-99.
2. Knight Rex and M. Knight, *A Modern Introduction to Psychology*, University Tutorial Press Ltd., Clifton House, London, 1957, p. 200.
3. M.N. Srinivas, *Changing Status of Indian Women*, Oxford University Press, London, 1978.
4. A. Shoma Chatterjee, *The Indian Women's Search for an Identity*, Vikas, New Delhi, 1988.
5. Saraswati Mishra, *Status of Indian Women*, Gyan Publications, New Delhi, 2002, pp. 181-82.
6. Sushila Jain, *Muslims and Modernization*, Rawat Publications, Jaipur and Delhi, 1986, p. 128-29.
7. Ibid., p. 118.
8. T. Parsons, *The Structure of Social Action*, The Free Press of Glencoe, 1961.
9. Yogendra Singh, *op. cit.*, p. 176.

10. Yogendra Singh, *Modernization of Indian Tradition*, Rawat Publications, Jaipur, 1988 (Reprint).
11. Louis Dumont, *Homo Hierarchicus: The Caste System and Its Implications*, Vikas, New Delhi, 1970.
12. Yogendra Singh, 1978, *op. cit.*, p. 182.
13. Ibid., pp. 182-84.
14. Ibid., pp. 179-80.
15. Michel Mann, *Sociology*, Macmillan Press, London, 1983, p. 112.
16. Yogendra Singh, *op. cit.*, p. 179.
17. Ibid., p. 180.
18. Michel Mann, *op. cit.*, p. 168.
19. Yogendra Singh, *op. cit.*, p. 180.
20. Ibid., p. 184.
21. Ibid., p. 180.
22. Michel Mann, *op. cit.*, p. 321.
23. Sumati Mulay and G.L. Roy, *Towards Modernization*, National, Delhi, 1973, p. 58.
24. Michel Mann, *op. cit.*, pp. 63-64.

7

Secularization and Religious Beliefs

According to Yogendra Singh, "rationality and secularism in the western cultural model imply a scientific-technological worldview which is essentially materialistic and probabilistic and is opposed to the principle of transcendence of the traditional culture".[1] Modernization implies a new awareness on the part of individuals, and on the part of society as a whole, regarding its environment which can be consciously directed on rational lines. It is one of the basic elements in the process of modernization.

Damle has explained the concept of secularism by providing a paradigm with the structural characteristics—rationality and emphasis on cognition, scientific spirit, individuation and individualism, universalism and freedom from particularistic loyalty of caste, kinship, religion and region, etc., rule of law and attainment of ethics.[2]

Damle writes: "The process of secularization offers an incentive to the growth and development of rationalism. It is because secularism is the hand-maid of modernism and modernism implies a breakthrough from the traditional social structure due to penetration of rationality into traditionalism."[3]

M.N. Srinivas uses the term secularization to imply "that what was formerly regarded as religious is ceasing to be such". This ceasing to be religious also implies "a process of differentiation which results in the various aspects of society, economic, political, legal and moral, becoming increasingly discrete in relation to each other. The distinction between Church and State, and the Indian conception of a secular state, both assume the existence of such differentiation".[4]

Mann[5] has analysed secularization in detail. Secularization is a contentious concept, largely because there is so little consensus as to what it is that constitutes religion.

Approaches to secularization broadly follow the two approaches to the definition of religion. Those who identify religion in terms of beliefs and actions oriented to supernatural beings (the substantive approach) regard secularization as the process in which the thought and behaviour of members of a society are less influenced by religious concerns, symbols and institutions. Such a notion does not entail the idea of a 'Golden Age of Faith' or a religious utopia in which society was fully religious compared to some other stage when it will become fully secular. It simply entails the presumption that at some point religious meanings, practices or institutions were more powerful than they are at some later point. Hence, this notion does not entail that secularization is unidirectional, nor that it is inevitable, although a number of thinkers (e.g., Freud, Frazer) have held this view. Secularization is not a unitary or unidimensional phenomenon. It has a number of different dimensions: changes in beliefs, practices, religious institutions and in other social institutions in the degree to which, for example, they have recourse to religious legitimations. Hence there will be different indicators of the process in different settings. While in Europe statistics on membership of religious institutions, or usages of their facilities, are often referred to in support of the claim that secularization has occurred, these are not the only indicators of secularization, nor are they even necessary. There is, therefore, no contradiction in the claim that England has become more secular and that this is shown by the declining numbers who belong to or attend the major Protestant churches, and the claim that the USA has become more secular even though the numbers of church members have increased through much of this century. Secularization can take different forms. In most European Protestant societies, and to a lesser extent in industrialized parts of Catholic Europe, church membership has declined dramatically; religious institutions have become less prominent; their personnel have lost status and authority, and supernatural beliefs have become less widely accepted though some, such as belief in God, retain significant support. In USA, there has been increasing church membership but many of these churches have become secular, defining their activities in terms of the provision of social facilities for integrating their members into the community and providing them with psychological support. In their beliefs the major American churches have become increasingly this-worldly, stressing the psychological comforts of religious belief, peace of mind, health and happiness, and adjustment.

While substantive approaches to religion regard secularization as having been a major feature of the development of advanced industrial societies, functional approaches to religion take a different view. They do not dispute that religious institutions and supernaturalistic beliefs have become less important in industrial societies. Functionalist theorists regard religion as a social universal. Every society has some set of common values (consensus) answering ultimate problems (see Functional theories of Religion) or providing meaning for the world of everyday life and a worldview whereby man's biological nature is transcended (see Invisible Religion). Religion may change its form but cannot disappear, nor even decline significantly. Religion in contemporary industrial societies is taking a new, less institutional, more individualistic, less theistic form, in which meaning is found in such themes as self-realization.

Substantive views of religion and secularization are usually informed by Weber's conception of the role of rationalization in the west (see Rationality, sense 2), of which secularization is one facet. Christianity, it is argued, was more prone to secularization in its early differentiation of the church and the world, the religious domain and the secular, liberating the profane world for rational scrutiny. Such distinctions are less readily made in Hindu or Buddhist cultures. Christianity, possessing a radically transcendent God, was also less magical in character than most world religions, and this rationalism was dramatically enhanced by the Reformation with its hostility to indulgences, penances, confession, and other beliefs and practices inhibiting the emergence of a fully rationalistic ethic and a demythologized cosmos.

The rationalizing effect of modern industrial production, particularly when combined with the disruption of traditional community, has been a powerful source of declining attachment to traditional religious beliefs and institutions. Industrial societies tend to be more secularized than agrarian societies; men more than women; working women more than housewives etc. Religion can remain particularly influential in a society when it becomes a focus for national or cultural identity, especially when faced with an external threat to that identity. Poland and Ireland display an extremely high level of continued commitment to the Catholic Church because of its role as a focus for resistance to the political and cultural imperialism of Russia and England.

Sacred and Secular

In order to analyse the term 'sacred', Loomis and Beegle[6] accepting Durkheim's definition mentioned sacred "as being a property not necessarily related to the intrinsic properties of persons, thoughts, and acts, but rather to the attitude people have towards them. The sacred is set apart by a particular attitude of respect. It is thought of as having peculiar virtues and social powers. Persons who come in contact with the sacred must assume special attitudes, respect and precautions. The sacred is hedged about by restrictions and taboos of all sorts ...However, when sacred persons, things or acts of any kind are used for utilitarian purposes, they become secularized, and people no longer hold the special reverential attitudes towards them that make them sacred". Significantly, Loomis and Beegle did not define sacred and secular, rather mentioned certain conditions of being sacred and secular. According to them, "if they are thought of as ways of maximizing returns and minimizing effort, they are secular and rational. If they are so respected and revered that violation results in a general emotional upheaval which may require retribution, they are sacred".[7]

Thus, for operational purposes, highly educated women were asked several questions asking them to state their degree of agreement and disagreement for each item question. On the basis of responses, the women were classified into five categories ranging from strongly sacred to strongly secular.

Belief in God

As regards belief in God, a majority of 83 percent of the women studied show the tendency towards being strongly sacred. 15 percent of the women show the tendency towards being sacred, whereas only 2 percent of women show neither sacred nor secular. It is significant that not even a single woman shows the tendency towards being strongly secular.

The study reveals that 78.4 percent of the women in the age group of 21 to 30, 81.2 percent of women in the age group of 31 to 40, 89.5 percent of women in the age group of 41 to 50 and 100 percent of women in the age group of 51 and above years show tendency towards strongly sacred values. Significantly, 16.9 percent of women in the age group of 21 to 30, 17.5 percent of women in the age group of 31 to 40, and 10.4 percent of women in the age group of 41 to 50 show a tendency towards sacred values. It means that highly educated women have faith in God.

Visit to Sacred Place

As regards the visit to sacred place or places, 66.5 percent of the women in the study show the tendency towards strongly sacred values. 31.5 percent of women show the tendency towards sacred values and only 2 percent of women neither show the tendency towards sacred nor secular values. It is significant that not a single woman show the tendency towards strongly secular values.

Rituals

As regards the rituals, 59 percent of the women studied show tendency towards strongly sacred, 39 percent of women show the tendency towards sacred and only 2 percent of women show the tendency towards neither sacred nor secular in relation to periodical rituals.

It is significant that not a single woman shows tendency towards strongly secular values in relation to periodical rituals, e.g., community, wide festivals and celebrations.

Rites of Passage

As regards the rites of passage, 47 percent of the women studied show tendency towards strongly sacred values, 33.5 percent of women show tendency towards sacred values, 15.5 percent of women show tendency towards neither sacred nor secular values and very significantly, and 4 percent of women show a tendency towards strongly secular values in relation to non-periodical rituals, e.g., rites of passage.

Tolerance

As regards the value of tolerance, only 9 percent of women show the tendency towards strongly sacred, whereas 14 percent of women show the tendency towards sacred values. 25.5 percent of women show the tendency towards neither sacred nor secular. Significantly, 51.5 percent of women show the tendency towards being strongly secular in relation to the value of tolerance.

It may be that the essence of all religions is the value of tolerance. The Hindu women are guided by the Hindu mythology, 'Sarve bhavantu sukhinah..' Women from the other religions are also guided by their own religion and religious beliefs.

Thus, it may be said that age, education as well as upbringing of a human being exert a considerable influence in determining the degree of sacred-secular values.

Notes

1. Yogendra Singh, *Essays on Modernization in India*, Manohar, New Delhi, 1978, p. 184.
2. Y.B. Damle, "Process of Secularization", in *Secularism its Implication for Law and Life* (ed.) by G.S. Sharma.
3. Ibid., p. 87.
4. M.N. Srinivas, *Social Change in Modern India*, University of California Press, Los Angeles, 1966.
5. Michel Mann, *Sociology*, Macmillan Press, London, 1983, pp. 346-47.
6. C.P. Loomis and J.A. Beegle, *Rural Social System*, New York: Prentice Hall, Inc., 1951.
7. Sumati Mulay and G.L. Ray, *Towards Modernization*, National, Delhi, 1973, p. 57.

8

Political Participation and Mass Media

Yogendra Singh has analysed political modernization as concept and process very scientifically and in a wide context. He writes: "We can review the literature on political modernization on the basis of two types of theoretical considerations: first, in regard to formulations concerning the nature and direction of this process emerging in different societal situations, and secondly, in terms of the conceptual components or variables that are used to determine the direction and process of modernization. In the first sense (nature and direction), the formulations concerning political modernization could either be 'evolutionary' or 'relativistic'. The evolutionary approach is based on the presuppositions that all societies will ultimately evolve a similar structural and cultural form of modernization, despite their historical dissimilarities, and that the historical factors will only determine the sequence of the evolutionary stages rather than their direction. The 'relativistic' approach, on the other hand, recognizes the possibility of divergent patterns in modernization owing to diversity of historical traditions.

On a conceptual basis or in terms of variables the treatment of political modernization can be classified as being 'systematic' or 'componental': the former being oriented to the analysis of modernization in terms of macro-structural variables and the latter trying to analyze this process with the help of isolated micro-level variables often selected for reasons of operational feasibility rather than architectonic coverage. The systematic approach may utilise groups, classes or even large-scale social systems such as national societies as units for analysis in modernization; or political modernization may be analyzed in the global perspective. The essential element in this type of analysis is the presupposition that modernization proceeds through transformations in the system as a whole and that the process operates teleologically towards its goal. On the other hand, the componential approach is usually focused on studying the interaction between selected variables that operationally define the process called 'political modernization' and which are arrived at by a process of abstraction from case histories of political modernization in various societies. Here too the unit of analysis may be a single society or a set of societies, but this is not relevant. What is relevant is the extent to which interdependence of variables is demonstrated to be generating or thwarting political modernization.

When we combine the above two sets of approaches to the analysis of modernization into a single paradigm, we get four types of orientation in the study of political modernization; these are: 'evolutionary-systematic', 'evolutionary-componental', 'relativistic-systematic' and 'relativistic-componental'."[1]

In the light of the above four approaches, it may be possible for us to evaluate which conceptual formulation is most relevant for analyzing the Indian phenomenon of political modernization. To our mind, the historical-relativistic formulation tends to be the most appropriate.

Yogendra Singh has further explained that "political modernization in the accepted sense of the term assumes universality of a political consensus based on political individualism or citizenship role. The organization of the political system through governmental and party administration, the communication of political values and ideologies, and the inter-play between various political groups, such as national and regional political elites, their followers, etc., are expected to be rationally constituted in bureaucracies through wider structural differentiation of political roles and statuses. Hence, a modern political structure is supposed to be not fused but differentiated, not holistic but individualistic, and not hierarchical but corporate. The question that arises is: how far is this conceptual model of modernization relevant for an analysis of political modernization in India? Is this implicit dichotomous formulation of structural differentiation a universal sociological reality? Social scientists have increasingly pointed out the simplistic assumptions that may be involved in such a view of modern structure".[2]

Singh further remarks that "modernization may not only involve progressive differentiation but also "de-differentiation" or fusion of roles at certain level of growth. But the more important bearing of this formulation lies in the corollary that it may not be necessary for all social systems to attempt to achieve the same degree of individualism, rationalism and specialization of roles in the political and other structures in order to realize the goal of political modernization".[3]

Singh has explained that "we intend to draw attention to a significant historical episode in Indian political life which, to our mind, did recognize the need for developing an alternative model for political modernization in conformity with the orthogenetic limitations of Indian society. This episode was the emergence of Gandhi on the Indian political horizon and his alternative to modernization".[4]

Structural Aspects of Political Modernization

Yogendra Singh writes: "An important structural change in India's political modernization which took place following Independence was the shift of emphasis from the mass-politics of Gandhi to the elite politics of Nehru. This elitism persisted purely as a result of structural constraints under which the political system had to function right from the village panchayats to parliament. It will be our purpose to analyze some of its ramifications and their bearing on the contemporary political process in India. For this, important structural isolates would be: (a) social structure and political party system; (b) social stratification and concentration of power and political resources at the levels of (i) caste, class and party, and (ii) elites and bureaucrats; (c) the growth of regionalism and regional disbalances; and finally, (d) structural compulsives of future trends in political modernization."[5]

Cultural Aspects of Political Modernization

Yogendra Singh has clearly explained the cultural aspects of political modernization. Singh writes: "The relationship between the Indian cultural tradition and political modernization can be understood through the extent to which established cultural institutions in India are concomitant with the political culture of modernization. The question immediately arises: how shall we define a modern political culture? In the contemporary literature on this subject, we find that modern political culture is equated with 'civic culture', to borrow the term from Sydney Verba and G. Almond, or it is equated with institutionalization of the universalistic norms of democratic associations. In both formulations, the notions of individual citizenship and civic rights and privileges based on constitutional guarantees are implicit. The enfranchisement of the citizens is only an extension of this principle of civic freedom. It is then postulated that, as traditional societies move towards political modernization, this concept of individual and citizenship roles emerges from the traditional background of communal and group-based solidarities and identities. The normative base of the culture of political modernity thus lies in the citizenship idea.

Yogendra Singh further remarks that "... right from the beginning of political modernization in India and the freedom struggle there existed an alternative political ideology concomitant with the normative attributes of the traditional Indian culture".

Yogendra Singh has mentioned three most important ideologies, e.g., democratic-liberalism, Marxism and Gandhism. The first two were of western origin and the last was an orthogenetic response. Singh writes: 'Gandhism was, however, inclusive of all the three cultural processes. It was a composite approach and should be treated as an alternative model for political and general modernization of Indian society'."[6]

Yogendra Singh analyzes that "the political culture which caught the imagination of the political elites in India was not the one suggested by Gandhi but one which was obtained as a legacy of colonialism with trimmings from the constitutional history of the Western nations. Its key values were welfare-socialism, secularism, individualism and rationalism. It was thus totally Western in idiom and ethos. Even secularism, which otherwise is older in Indian tradition than the West, was acknowledged in its Western form of religious neutrality rather than transcendence and fusion of religions at a higher level".[7]

Yogendra Singh further writes: "In what direction then has political culture developed in India? We find that it has fully corresponded with structural changes and its tendencies; in other words, liberal democratic culture (in the Western sense) even today exists only in a sub-cultural form, and the wider political spectrum has involved an altogether different equation of modernity with tradition which is rooted in the status principle of stratification."[8]

Political Participation

According to Yogendra Singh, "the relevant issues in the process of Indian political modernization at the macro-structural level are regarding the nature of formation of political parties, emergence of political leadership, the role of bureaucracy (administrative, managerial and military) in the political processes and the functioning of the federal politics and finally its cultural integration through communication media (linguistic media), value systems and ideologies. At the micro-structural level the aspects of political modernization involve problems of caste and ethnic politics, patterns of voting behaviour, and the role of regionalism and sub-regionalism in politics. It may not be possible for us to deal with all these aspects of political modernization in India in this short space, but it is necessary to keep all these dimensions in mind in a systematic analysis of the problem".[9]

Inkeles has described participant syndrome as:

(1) freedom from traditional authority. Identification with and allegiance to leaders and organizations transcending the parochial and primordial;
(2) interest in public affairs validated by keeping informed and expressed through participation in civic action; and
(3) orientation toward political and governmental processes which recognizes and accepts the necessity and desirability of a rational structure of rules and regulations.[10]

According to Inkeles, "this syndrome is one any modern man might be expected to manifest, just as any modern polity is likely to desire, perhaps even require, that he possess it".[11]

Those who are familiar with the civic culture will recognize these traits as very similar to those delineated by Almond and Verba as defining the model of a democratic citizen. According to them,[12] the citizen of democratic polity is expected to:

(1) engage in political discussion;
(2) take interest in politics;
(3) vote;
(4) have knowledge of politics;
(5) express a general sense of competence to influence the government; and
(6) Participate in civic affairs.

In short, the stress is on 'activity, involvement and rationality'.

Milbrath[13] has presented a conceptual analysis of political involvement which includes the activities:

(1) voting;
(2) discussion and opinion leadership;

(3) wearing a button or putting a sticker on the car;
(4) petitioning political leaders;
(5) making a monetary contribution;
(6) attending a political meeting;
(7) active party membership;
(8) campaigning;
(9) soliciting political funds;
(10) office-seeking and holding; and
(11) Protests and demonstrations.

Thus, an attempt has been made to find out the relationship between political participation and the process of modernization in relation to the present study. It is divided into five areas: (1) political discussions, (2) political activity, (3) voting, (4) organizational membership, and (5) membership of a political party.

Political Discussions

In societies where modern channels of communication and mass media are not readily available to citizens, the interpersonal channels of word-of-mouth communication from family members, neighbours, friends, school teachers, and extension agents are very important in order to affect the receiver's knowledge, attitudes and behaviour in desired ways.[14] "Mass media communication is more important in changing cognitions whereas interpersonal communication is more likely to cause attitude change. When the object is persuasion, word-of-mouth channels would seem preferable to the mass media."[15] If ordinary men and women are to participate in a democratic political process, they must have the feeling that it is safe to do so, that they do not assume great risks when they express political opinions and they can be relatively free about the person to whom they talk.[16]

As regards, age and political discussions, the study reveals that 13 percent of women like to discuss political issues everyday. About 28.5 percent of women like to discuss political issues once a week, 51 percent of women like to discuss political issues from time to time. Only 7.5 percent of women do not like to discuss political issues.

The study also reveals that 16.9 percent of women in the age group of 21 to 30, 13.7 percent of women in the age group of 31 to 40, 6.2 percent of women in the age group of 41 to 50 and 14.2 percent of women in the age group of 51 years and above like to discuss political issues everyday. Around 32.3 percent of women in the age group of 21 to 30, 55 percent of women in the age group of 31 to 40, 50 percent of women in the age group of 41 to 50 and 28.5 percent of women in the age group of 51 years and above like to discuss political issues once a week. Around 44.6 percent of women in the age group of 21 to 30, 50 percent of women in the age group of 31 to 40, 62.5 percent of women in the age group of 41 to 50 and 42.8 percent of women in the age group of 51 years and above like to discuss political issues from time to time. Only 6.1 percent of women in the age group of 21 to 30, 8.7 percent of women in the age group of 31 to 40, 6.2 percent of women in the age group of 41 to 50 and 14.2 percent of women in the age group of 51 years and above do not like to discuss political issues. It is significant that the frequency of political discussion not only indicates the citizens' confidence in the democratic process but also suggests her openness to other ideas.

As regards caste and political discussions, 11.6 percent of women from the higher castes, 15.5 percent of women from the middle castes, 15 percent of women from the lower castes and 13.3 percent of women from other religions like to discuss political issues everyday. About 25 percent of women from the higher castes, 31.1 percent of women from the middle castes, 35 percent of women from the lower castes and 40 percent of women from other religions like to discuss political issues once a week. Around 57.5 percent of women from the higher castes, 44.4 percent of women from the middle castes, 35 percent of women from the lower castes and 40 percent of women from other religions like to discuss political issues from time to time. Only 5.8 percent of women from the higher castes, 8.8 percent of women from the middle castes, 15 percent of women from the lower castes and 6.6 percent of women from other religions do not like to discuss political issues.

Political Activity

In the study, it is significant to note not only how frequently women talked about politics but also the kinds of activities they indulged in and how they participated in these activities. Almond and Verba writes: "Citizens differ not only in how much activities they engage in but also in the type of activity, and that this difference in type represents significant variations in the ways citizens attempt to influence government and the types of issues that lead them to become inactive".[17]

As regards engaging in political activity, 8.5 percent of women like to engage themselves in active political meetings, 7 percent of women like to engage themselves in political campaign but the majority of women (84.5%) do not like to participate in these political activities.

As regards age and political activities, the study reveals that 7.6 percent of women in the age group of 21 to 30, 8.7 percent of women in the age group of 31 to 40, 8.3 percent of women in the age group of 41 to 50 and 14.2 percent of women in the age group of 51 years and above like to engage themselves in political meetings. Around 7.6 percent of women in the age group of 21 to 30, 6.2 percent of women in the age group of 31 to 40, 6.2 percent of women in the age group of 41 to 50 and 14.2 percent of women in the age group of 51 years and above like to engage themselves in campaigning for parties. While 84.6 percent of women in the age group of 21 to 30, 85 percent of women in the age group of 31 to 40, 85.4 percent of women in the age group of 41 to 50 and 71.4 percent of women in the age group of 51 years and above neither like to engage in political meetings nor in campaigning for political parties.

As regards the castes and political activities, 5.8 percent of women from the higher castes, 11.1 percent of women from the middle castes, 15 percent women from the lower castes and 13.3

percent of women from other religions like to engage themselves in political meetings, 5 percent of women from the higher castes, 11.1 percent from the middle castes, 10 percent of women from the lower castes and 6.6 percent of women from other religions like to engage themselves in political campaigning. But, 89.1 percent of women from the higher castes, 77.7 percent of women from the middle castes, 75 percent of women from the lower castes and 80 percent of women from other religions do not like to engage in these political activities.

Voting

Rajni Kothari has explained that "the roles of adult franchise and periodic elections have been pivotal, not only in displacing the principle of hierarchy but also in establishing a unified focus of attention and affect for the vast masses of people, even before the other learning processes of education and urbanization begin to play their role".[18] Every individual in a democratic system may have an intention and pre-disposition to vote which is indicative of a particular kind of orientation towards the election system as a whole.

On the issue of the participation of women in the voting system, since 59.5 percent of women cast their vote regularly, they are placed in the category of high participation. While 25.5 percent of women cast their vote in the elections but not regularly and they are placed in the category of medium participation, 10.5 percent of women cast their vote occasionally and they are placed in the category of low participation. Only 4.5 percent of women are apathetic towards voting in the elections and they placed in the category of apathetic.

As regards age and participation of women in the voting system, 63 percent of women in the age group of 21 to 30, 66.2 percent of women in the age group of 31 to 40, 47.9 percent of women in the age group of 41 to 50 and 28.5 percent of women in the age group of 51 years and above cast their vote regularly. While 21.5 percent of women in the age group of 21 to 30, 20 percent of women in the age group of 31 to 40, 37.5 percent of women in the age group of 41 to 50 and 42.8 percent of women in the age group of 51 years and above cast their vote but not regularly. About 10.7 percent of women in the age group of 21 to 30, 10 percent of women in the age group of 31 to 40, 10.4 percent of women in the age group of 41 to 50 and 42.8 percent of women in the age group of 51 years and above cast their vote occasionally. Only 4.6 percent of women in the age group of 21 to 30, 43.7 percent of women in the age group of 31 to 40, 4.1 percent of women in the age group of 41 to 50 and 14.2 percent of women in the age group of 51 and above years are apathetic towards voting in the elections.

Organizational Membership

Almond and Verba writes: "These associations help him avoid the dilemma of being either a parochial, cut off from political influence, or an isolated and powerless individual, manipulated and mobilized by the mass institutions of politics and government. The availability of his primary groups as a political resource. Membership in voluntary associations gives him a more structured set of political resources, growing out of his varied interests."[19]

According to Hall, "participation in voluntary organizations helps in generating self-confidence. A self-confident citizen is also a modern citizen".[20]

As regards the membership of organizations, 51.5 percent of women were the members of social organization(s), whereas 23.5 percent of the women in the study were members of economic organization(s). It is significant that most of the organization were religious and women dominated.

As regards age and membership of the organization, 27.6 percent of women in the age group of 21 to 30, 55 percent of women in the age group of 31 to 40, 56.2 percent of women in the age group of 41 to 50 and 57.1 percent of women in the age group of 51 years and above are the members of the social organization(s). Whereas, 10.7 percent of women in the age group of 21 to 30, 25 percent of women in the age group of 31 to 40, 35.4 percent of women in the age group of 41 to 50 and 57.1 percent of women in the age group of 51 years and above are members of economic/professional organization(s).

As regards castes and the membership of the organization, 58.3 percent of women from the higher castes, 55.5 percent of women from the middle castes, 25 percent of women from the lower castes and 20 percent of women from the other religions are members of social organization(s). In comparison, 23.3 percent of women from the higher castes, 68.8 percent of women from the middle castes, 90 percent of women from the lower castes and 15 percent of women from the other religions are members of economic/professional organization(s). Economic organizations which are established by the government are also included in the category of economic organizations.

Membership of a Political Party

It is very significant here to quote Yogendra Singh: "The process of political party formation within the operative norms of democracy is itself an indicator of modernization. Parties are otherwise groups that are societalized, that is, they are oriented to a goal (acquisition of power) in a planned manner and based on a rational order (distribution of administrative offices, rights and responsibilities among the staff and the functionaries, etc.), and in this sense parties involve communal action which they can mobilize either on a class basis or on the basis of status groups like castes and tribes and religious communities. Parties based entirely on communal or status group structure were always there in the eastern and the western societies, but these did not contribute to political modernization as in terms of their operation they soon degenerated either into pressure groups, private armies or factions. Modern political parties only emerged with the inception of industrial society and its rational equalitarian order; in Europe their fuller growth coincided with the breakdown in the 'estates' which have status groups; it is coincided with the process which removed the hierarchical and closed system of stratification".[21]

Milbrath has explained that "there are three ways in which a person could be said to be a party affiliate or member: (a) psychological identification with a party; (b) formal membership through payment of dues; and (c) active participation in party affairs. Psychological identification means that the person likes the party and is inclined to support it with a vote at election time".[22]

The study reveals that 35.5 percent of women are the members of a political party. It shows that women are not much conscious about membership in a political party. It also shows that the political parties are failing to protect the aspirations of the women.

As regards the age of women and the membership of a political party, 38.4 percent of women in the age group of 21 to 30, 33.7 percent of women in the age group of 31 to 40, 35.4 percent of women in the age group of 41 to 50 and 28.5 percent of women in the age group of 51 years and above are members of the political parties.

As regards the caste of women and membership of a political party, 29.1 percent of women from the higher castes, 44.4 percent of women from the middle castes, 60 percent of women from the lower castes and 26.6 percent of women from other religions are members of the political parties.

Mass Media

Mass media are an important variable in the process of modernization in developing societies. Lerner writes: "Increasingly, in the villages and hamlets of the world, the mass media are bringing 'strange new worlds' into the traditional environment of the rural people."[23] In traditional societies, awareness of modern political roles (political socialization) comes in part from experience with the mass media system, since media are a major purveyor of modern influences. Lerner notes that public communication activates new modes of socialization. A new political class is recruited that aggregates new interests.

The nature and scope of the mass media differs from one country to another. In the communication process in transitional societies, the urban and the village levels are not closely integrated. In less developed countries, mass media reach only a small audience, such as university students, members of professions, the middle class, and urban dwellers. This is due to the limited availability, and the degree of government control. Communication can be direct or indirect, through face to face contact versus the impersonal channels. Recent years have shown a tremendous growth in mass media techniques. Using these new techniques such as radio and television, the government of developing countries are reaching large audiences.

Rogers and Svenning writes: "Larger mass media audiences, accompanied by high levels of mass media exposure per capita, can be expected to lead those exposed to more favourable attitudes towards change and development, to greater awareness of political events and to more knowledge of technical information". It is found that mass media correlate with other variables of modernization such as literacy, political knowledge, empathy, innovativeness, aspirations, and achievement motive.[24]

Yogendra Singh has analysed the changes in traditional cultural practices and institutions. According to Singh, "the changes in traditional cultural practices and institutions are closely related to the process of urbanization, patterns of migration, politicization of caste and community relationships in villages and the rapid pace of growth and expansion of the electronic media of information and entertainment throughout the country".[25]

In this study, women were asked about the type of mass media and frequency of their exposure to television, cinema, radio, newspapers, magazines and computer (internet).

Television

Television is the most popular and powerful media in our society. At first, Doordarshan started several programmes but now the cable and satellite system have captured the market of urban population in India.

Yogendra Singh writes: "The mass media, particularly the television which is rapidly penetrating the domains of leisure, are envisaged to project images of person, culture and society to reinforce humanistic social and economic development of society. Its symbols and messages are expected to help in developing a modern, just, prosperous and harmonious society. The richer elements of India's traditional heritages drawn from all regions, communities and groups are to be articulated to show their ever-lasting relevance. Despite there being some evidence that these objectives remain on the agenda of television, the encroachment of consumerist values and market culture in its programmes generates scepticism. It is evident that uneven social development has enhanced the power of the rich to control the institution of mass culture and its pattern of leisure. Relying heavily on mass media for promotion of leisure would logically mean increasing the control of these classes on leisure and culture of society. It would threaten and rupture the cultural and social objectives of modernization of our society."[26]

The study reveals that 43 percent of women view television regularly, 27 percent of women view television a number of times a week, 15 percent of women view television at least once a week, 7.5 percent of women view television occasionally and 7 percent of women never watch television.

As regards the age of women and the frequency of television viewing, 43 percent of women in the age group of 21 to 30, 48.7 percent of women in the age group of 31 to 40, 37.5 percent of women in the age group of 41 to 50 and 14.2 percent of women in the age group of 51 years and above view television regularly. About 30.7 percent of women in the age group of 21 to 30, 25 percent of women in the age group of 31 to 40, 29.1 percent of women in the age group of 41 to 50 and 14.2 percent of women in the age group of 51 years and above view television a number of times a week. While 16.9 percent of women in the age group of 21 to 30, 16.2 percent of women in the age group of 31 to 40, 10.4 percent of women in the age group of 41 to 50 and 14.2 percent of women in the age group of 51 years and above view television at least once a week. Around 9.2 percent of women in the age group of 21 to 30, 5 percent of women in the age group of 31 to 40, 6.2 percent of women in the age group of 41 to 50 and 28.5 percent of women in the age group of 51 years and above view television occasionally. It is evident that women in the age group of 21 to 30 view television but 5 percent of women in the age group of 31 to 40, 16.6 percent of women in the age group of 41 to 50 and 28.5 percent of women in the age group of 51 years and above do not watch television.

Cinema

Cinema is a powerful media of mass communication. The Government of India produces documentaries which are shown before the movie starts.

As regards the frequency of cinema viewing, the study reveals that 6.5 percent of women see films regularly. Around 15 percent of women go to the cinema a number of times a month. About 26.5 percent of women view cinema at least once a year. Almost 40 percent of women go to the cinema occasionally and 12 percent of women are not interested in this media.

As regards the age of women and the frequency of cinema viewing, 9.2 percent of women in the age group of 21 to 30, 5 percent of women in the age group of 31 to 40 and 6.2 percent of women in the age group of 41 to 50 go to the cinema regularly. It is evident that women in the age group of 51 years and above are not very interested in this media. About 16.9 percent of women in the age group of 21 to 30, 16.2 percent of women in the age group of 31 to 40 and 12.5 percent of women in the age group of 41 to 50 go to the cinema a number of times a month. 30.7 percent of women in the age group of 21 to 30, 25 percent of women in the age group of 31 to 40, 25 percent of women in the age group of 41 to 50 and 14.2 percent of women in the age group of 51 years and above view cinema at least once a year. 43 percent of women in the age group of 21 to 30, 43.7 percent of women in the age group of 31 to 40, 33.3 percent of women in the age group of 41 to 50 and 14.2 percent of women in the age group of 51 years and above view cinema occasionally. 10 percent of women in the age group of 31 to 40, 22.9 percent of women in the age group of 41 to 50 and 71.4 percent of women who are 51 years and above are not very interested in this media.

Radio

The radio is a popular media in our society. But now, in urban areas, it is losing its importance. It is significant that the radio is still popular among women in comparison to men. The study reveals that 13 percent of women listen to the radio regularly. 16 percent of women listen to the radio a number of times a week. Around 26.5 percent of women listen to the radio at least once a week. While 37 percent of women listen to the radio occasionally and 5 percent of women are not interested in listening to the radio programmes.

As regards the age of women and the frequency of radio listening, 9.2 percent of women in the age group of 21 to 30, 5 percent of women in the age group of 31 to 40, 25 percent of women in the age group of 41 to 50 and 57.1 of women in the age group of 51 years and above listen to the radio regularly. About 12.3 percent of women in the age group of 21 to 30, 16.2 percent of women in the age group of 31 to 40, 20.8 percent of women in the age group of 41 to 50 and 14.2 percent of women in the age group of 51 years and above listen to the radio a number of times a week. Around 30.7 percent of women in the age group of 21 to 30, 31.2 percent of women in the age group of 31 to 40, 25 percent of women in the age group of 41 to 50 and 14.2 percent of women in the age group of 51 years and above listen to the radio at least once a week. 41.5 percent of women in the age group of 21 to 30, 45 percent of women in the age group of 31 to 40, 20.8 percent of women in the age group of 41 to 50 and 14.2 percent of women in the age group of 51 years and above listen radio occasionally. Around 6.1 percent of women in the age group of 21 to 30, 2.5 percent in the age group of 31 to 40 and 8.3 percent of women in the age group of 41 to 50 are not interested in listening to the radio programmes.

Newspapers

The study reveals that 82.5 percent of women claimed to be regular readers of newspapers. While 9 percent of women read the newspapers a number of times a week. About 5.5 percent of women claimed to be weekly readers of newspapers while 3 percent of women read the newspapers only occasionally. It is significant that in the study all women read newspapers. It is also significant that all women in the age group of 21 to 30 are regular readers of newspapers.

Magazines

As regards magazines, the study reveals that 79 percent of women read magazines devoted to public affairs regularly. Nearly 10 percent of women read these magazines a number of times a week. Around 6 percent of women read these magazines at least once a week and 5 percent are just occasional readers. It is evident that all the women in the age group of 21 to 30 are regular readers of magazines. It is also significant that all women read these magazines.

Mass Media Exposure and Government Policies and Actions

The women were asked about their perception of governmental policies, programmes, actions and the extent of support given to governmental policies and actions. Hence, several questions were put to the women, such as "how much effect do you think people like you have on what the government does?

Do you have some influence, or a great deal of influence or no influence? In general, how well do you think the national government understands the needs of the people of this country; does it understand them well or not so well?"

In this study, an attempt was made to find a correlation, if any, between the extent of public support, perception of governmental policies and actions and the level of mass media exposure. The study reveals that 52.5 percent of women who are highly exposed to mass media are also high supporters of the governmental policies and actions while 34 percent of moderately exposed women generally provide moderate support to governmental policies and actions. Only 13.5 percent low exposed women give low support to the governmental policies and actions.

Though the role of mass media in developing political cognitions and knowledge is widely accepted, its contribution to political development and modernization is indispensable. It makes "indispensable inputs to the psycho-political life of a transitional society via the minds and hearts of its people". Communication is the crux of modernization. It helps persons to become participants and modern.[27]

Notes

1. Yogendra Singh, *Essays on Modernization*, Manohar, New Delhi, 1978, pp. 40-41.
2. Ibid., pp. 44-45.
3. Ibid., p. 46.
4. Ibid., p. 47.
5. Ibid., p. 49.
6. Ibid., pp. 57-59.
7. Ibid., pp. 59-60.
8. Ibid., p. 60.
9. Ibid., p. 67.

10. Alex Inkeles, "Participant Citizenship in Six Developing Countries", *American Political Science Review*, LXIII, 1969, p. 11-22.
11. Ibid., p. 11-22.
12. D.K. Vajpeyi, *Modernization and Social Change in India*, Manohar, New Delhi, 1979, p. 73.
13. Ibid., pp. 74-75.
14. Ibid., pp. 74-75.
15. E. Rogers, *Diffusion of Innovations*, New York: Free Press, 1962.
16. G. Almond and Sidney Verba, *The Civic Culture*, Princeton, N.J.: Princeton University Press, 1963.
17. Ibid., p. 93.
18. Rajni Kothari, "Congress System on Trial", *Asian Survey*, 1970, p. 283.
19. Almond and Verba, *op. cit.*, p. 245.
20. Peter M. Hall, "Identification with the Delinquent Subculture and level of Self-evaluation", *Sociometry*, 29, No. 2, 1966, p. 147.
21. Yogendra Singh, *op. cit.*, p. 67.
22. Lester W. Milbrath, *Political Participation*, Chicago: Rand McNally and Co., 1965, p. 3.
23. Daniel Lerner, "International Cooperation and Communication", in *National Development*, Lerner and Schramm (eds.), 1967, pp. 122-23.
24. D.K. Vajpeyi, *op. cit.*, pp. 159-60.
25. Yogendra Singh, *Culture Change in India: Identity and Globalization*, Rawat Publications, Jaipur and New Delhi, 2000, p. 18.
26. Ibid., pp. 235-36.
27. D.K. Vajpeyi, *op. cit.*, p. 198.

9

Conclusion

According to Yogendra Singh, "tradition and modernity as heuristic concepts are easy to formulate, but to separate them at substantive level is rather difficult. Modernization, as a process, in fact, has more elasticity of form than tradition. It implies an open worldview which like science undergoes perpetual self-falsification and self-transcendence in its value-structure and postulates".[1]

The two concepts which have often been counterposed in the debate on the ideology of social change are westernization and modernization. This debate runs through the entire gamut of the various movements for cultural renaissance of India since the beginning of the British rule. It permeates the value of our national leadership during the freedom movement.[2]

Yogendra Singh has explained: "Is modernization without westernization possible? In what sense are the two terms conceptually distinct? Could one outline concrete indicators of the two processes to measure differences? Social scientists in India have debated these points for several decades. Sometimes, a distinction between modernization and westernization is made on the basis that westernization is an empirically observable phenomenon in the behaviour and lifestyle of the people whereas modernization is an ideological concept. However, it is not easy to spell out the characteristics of modernization as an ideology. Modernization is a form of rationalization through which introduction of a whole range of social and cultural changes in societies is legitimated. Social scientists have worked out empirical indicators of modernization. These too, however, remain in the realm of rationalization since even to this date no universally accepted sets of modernization indicators exist. Now, even the notion of modernity is being challenged and seems to be on the retreat."[3]

Singh states: "The challenges that traditional cultural values are facing in India today relate to the contradictions between the old and the new worldviews and culture norms and the extent to which the selective adaptation in the older-values is taking place in the wake of the new values. For this adaptation the changes in social structure play a crucial role. The new cultural values, of egalitarianism, social justice, secularism, legal rationalism, democracy and planned transformation of society have deeper implications for transformation in the social structure of Indian society, and to a large measure are dependent upon the realization of this transformation. Karl Mannheim characterized this feature of the crisis in the contemporary western cultures as the 'contemporaneity of the non-contemporaneous' where the norms of the old and the new order of culture exist in a random non-syncretic fashion. Here the contradictions are primarily symbolic and cognitive. For the developing countries, especially India, the challenges to culture are linked more primarily to structural contradictions than to lags in the symbolic and cognitive universe of the people. The latter may be existent but more because of the inelasticity of the social structure. The contradictions between values of hierarchy versus equality, holism versus individualism, continuity versus historicity and transcendence versus techno-scientific rationalism are not merely culturological but are imbued with critical structural implications.

No doubt, India has made significant advances since independence in evolving an operational cultural policy of pluralism but the emphasis on pluralism has also been instrumental to some extent in not being adequately responsive to the poor man's 'culture of silence'. This contradiction may sometimes evoke in over-wrought minds the fantasy of a culture of *fanshen* or revolutionary transformation. In the Indian context, however, it is symptomatic of the intensity of cultural crisis than its real or possible solution.

Let us examine the concrete forces behind this crisis. The emphasis on the culture of equality combined with historicity has a tendency to assume apocalyptic symbolic and cognitive significance to generate demands for socio-cultural transformation in society much beyond its capacity to manage orderly social change. This type of cognitive universe is typical of the middle class intelligentsia in developing societies. Also, in India today, we may be witnessing a similar crisis of contradiction between the value of *equality* and *historicity*. A cognitive history has emerged between the capacity of the cultural system to respond meaningfully or systematically to the process of change and the expectations of the desired quantum of change. Institutions of adult franchise, high degree of media exposure, verbalization of egalitarian ideology with emphasis on planned transformation of society, have generated expectations among people which have got transfigurated into psychologically charged symbols of status achievement commensurate with which concrete changes in social structure have not taken place. There is not merely a contradiction building up between expectation and achievement but also between 'fantasy' and reality. Historicity implies a collective value orientation for the desirability of '*here and now*' transformation of social situations by human effort: It involves commitment of collective will and collective mobilization of values or at least acquiescence to these values. In Indian democracy such values have remained refracted due to the uneven pattern of social mobility, and relative growth in the rigidity of class structure of society. This development does not reinforce cultural historicity but either social 'parasitism' or cultural vulgarity. Under its pressure the authenticity of folk cultures, rich native styles and symbolic media are lost in the wane hope of their new self-transformation which is never achieved.

At the base of this contradiction are the dilemmas of combination of the new and old cultural values on the one hand and the constraints of social structure realities of Indian society on the other. The type of cultural policy which India requires to achieve its cultural commitments would be that of working out a synthesis among the values of equality, historicity and holism with collectivity orientation. But the realities of the Indian pattern of social stratification, composition and culture of elites and the nature of power structure create culture demands which tend to push the value-configuration towards a synthesis of historicity with rational individualism—the hall mark of the culture of a capitalist society. Here lies the basic contradiction of the contemporary Indian cultural values whose ramifications are many and could be analysed separately."[4]

There are a number of attributes associated with highly educated women, which are helpful in the process of modernization. The exposure to urban area, higher education up to doctoral level, media exposure, participation in politics and change, the campus environment, exposure to the system of co-education and employment are some of the basic factors favouring a modern outlook and development of a rational outlook and approach. But at the same, there are certain attributes associated with this section of society, which are traditional in nature.

Indian women have been subject to social exploitation for centuries. They were destined to serve the male members in the society throughout their life. In the pre-marital period, it was obligatory for them to serve their fathers; after marriage they were required to serve their husbands and later they were required to serve their sons also. Their activities were confined to the four walls of their home. They were not allowed to move freely and to take part in the educational, political, economic and industrial affairs of life. Outdoor participation was an exclusive privilege for men. The religious and traditional sanctions prohibited them from performing certain sacred rites and on certain occasions they were treated as 'polluted'. Consequently, women in Indian society remained dominated by religious orthodoxy and traditional conservatism. In such a situation, a rational outlook could not be developed among the women of traditional Indian society. But today the situation is changing.

The highly educated women stand at the junction of tradition and modernity. The family background and traditional heritage pull them towards traditionalism whereas education, job, urbanism, participation in politics and media exposure push them towards modernity. The personal and family structures of these highly educated women are exposing them to more and more modern forces. The urban setting has helped them in having a greater degree of exposure to the social structure undergoing the process of rationalization. They live with their husbands and children. Hence, they are free to a greater extent in enjoying personal liberty and in managing their family affairs according to their own approach and outlook. The break-away from the traditional joint family has helped them in enjoying a greater degree of liberty. In this way, higher educational and economic statuses of women result in more authority for women and now they are taking important decisions regarding money matters within their families. It was found that due to the new roles, there is a definite change in the status of women. Now, women have a greater say in the decision-making structure of the family and the higher the economic status of women, the greater is their say in the family decision. Moreover, this break-away from the traditional joint family system is in itself an index of modernity. Highly educated women do not find any clash or conflict in the performance of their two roles—the job role and the domestic role, but it depends upon the pattern of adjustment and the question of social conditioning. There is a positive relationship between the reason of work and the patterns of adjustment. There was no such role-conflict between spouses due to the job, but the role and the attitude of husband are very significant in this matter. Women these days, are satisfied with their performance of job role and they also perform their role as mothers very satisfactorily.

Women now hold a modern attitude and they are in favour of equality between women and men. The economic role has earned them equality of status but this role has not earned them any relief from household duties. The educational opportunities and employment of women does create new attitudes but not a total change in the attitudes of women.

There is no doubt education, occupation and age exert a considerable influence in determining the levels of aspirations and degrees of adopting of values.

The participation in politics of highly educated women is still not very high. Whenever they tried to participate actively or join organizations, they select those organizations which are mainly traditional, or religious. The messages carried by the mass media affect the women's information level and shape her cognition of various important factors—essential to making her a participant individual and thereby generating social and political change.

Women are exposed to a number of modern factors and forces. They are not dominantly traditional in their manners and ways. Their habits, manners and ways of life are very different from traditional patterns. They enjoy modern amenities and their adaptation to the modern material world has changed their manners, ways and behaviour to 'others'.

Thus, this changing trend leads us to draw the conclusion that a process of tradition-modernity continuum exists (here, Yogendra Singh's explanation of tradition-modernity continuum in relation to Indian society is empirically proved). The highly educated women are dominantly rational and modern in their outlook and behaviour to 'others', though the actual practice is lagging slightly behind their current ideas and attitudes.

Notes

1. Yogendra Singh, *Modernization of Indian Tradition*, Rawat Publications, Jaipur, 1988(Reprint), p. 121.
2. Yogendra Singh, *Culture Change in India: Identity and Globalization*, Rawat Publications, Jaipur and New Delhi, 2000, pp. 106-7.
3. Ibid., pp. 107-8.
4. Yogendra Singh, *Essays on Modernization in India*, Manohar, New Delhi, 1978, 187-89.

Bibliography

Adyantha, N.K., "Women's Employment in India", *International Review*, July, 1954.

Agnew, Vijay, *Elite Women in Indian Politics*, Vikas Publishing House, New Delhi, 1979.

Almond, G.A. and Sidney Verba, *The Civic Culture*, Boston and Toronto: Little Brown and Co., 1965.

Amin, Samir, *Unequal Development*, Oxford University Press, New Delhi, 1979.

Amin, U., "The Acceptance of Equality", *Seminar*, 52: 1963.

Anand, Kulwant, "Attitudes of Panjabi University Women Students Towards Marriage and Family", *Indian Journal of Social Work*, 26.

Anuradha and Muni, S.D., "Tradition vs Modernity: Women in Nepal and Sri Lanka", in *Women of the World* (eds.), Urmilla Phadnis and Indira Malani, Vikas, New Delhi, 1978.

Apter, David, *Politics of Modernization*, Chicago: University of Chicago Press, 1965.

Arora, K.K., Bhattacharya and Others, "Women and Career", a group project report submitted to the Tata Institute of Social Sciences, Bombay, 1963.

Asthana, P., *Women's Movement in India*, Vikas, New Delhi, 1974.

Atal, Y. and Mishra, Rajesh, *Understanding the Social Sphere: The Village and Beyond*, Rawat Publications, Jaipur and New Delhi, 2004.

Awasthi, A., (ed.), *Modernity, Feminism and Women's Empowerment*, Rawat Publications, Jaipur and New Delhi, 2001.

Bajaj, Neelam, "Job Involvement in High and Low Anxious Working Women", *Journal of Psychological Research*, Vol. 22 (I), 1978.

Bakshi, B.P., "Changing Role and the Status of Women in Society", *Social Welfare*, 11: 1, 1964.

Banfield, Edward C., *The Moral Basis of a Backward Society*, Glencoe Illinois: The Free Press, 1958.

Baudrillard, Jean, *Simulacres et Simulation*, Paris: Galilee, 1981.

Bauman, Zygmunt, "Sociological Response to Post-modernity", Thesis Eleven, 1989.

Beauvoir, S. de, *The Second Sex*, Penguin, London, 1953.

Beig, Tara, *Women of India*, S. Chand and Co., New Delhi, 1958.

—, *India's Women Power*, S. Chand and Co., New Delhi, 1976.

Bellah, R.N., "Religion and Progress in Modern Asia", *American Sociological Review*, Vol. 33, No. 3, 1964.

Bendix, Reinhart, *Nation-building and Citizenship*, John Wiley and Sons, Inc., New York, 1964.

Beteille, A., "The Position of Women in Indian Society", in *Indian Women* (ed.), Publication Division, New Delhi, 1975.

Bhasin, Kamla and Nighat Said Khan, *Some Questions on Feminism and Its Relevance*, Kali for Women, New Delhi, 1986.

Bhoite, Anuradha, *Women Employees and Rural Development*, Gian Publishing House, Delhi, 1987.

Black, C.E., *The Dynamics of Modernization*, Harper and Row, New York, 1967.

Boserup, Ester, *Women's Role in Economic Development*, George Allen and Unwin Ltd., London, 1970.

Brijbhushan, Jamila, *Muslim Women in Purdah and Out of It*, Vikas, New Delhi.

Buck and Jacobson, "Social Evolution and Structural-Functional Analysis: An Empirical Test", *American Sociological Review*, Vol. 33, No. 3, 1968.

Chadha, G.R., *WTO and the Indian Economy*, (ed.), Deep and Deep Publications Pvt. Ltd., New Delhi, 2001.

Chafe, W.H., *Women and Equality: Changing Pattern of American Culture*, Oxford University Press, New Delhi, 1977.

Chekki, D.A., *Modernization and Kin Network*, Leiden: E.J. Brill, 1974.

Chaki-Sircar, M., *Feminism in a Traditional Society: Women of the Manipur Valley*, Shakti Books, Vikas, New Delhi, 1984.

Chakravarty, K., *Conflicting Worlds of Working Mothers: A Sociological Inquiry*, Progress Publications, Calcutta, 1978.

Chakravarty, R., "The Working Women", *Seminar*, No. 52, December, 1963.

Chandra, Bipin, "Colonialism and Modernization", paper presented at the 32nd Indian History Congress, Jabalpur, 1970.

Channa, Karuna, *Socialization, Education and Women: Exploration in Gender Identity*, (ed.), Orient Longman Ltd., Hyderabad, 1988.

—, *Interrogating Women's Education: Bounded Visions*, Expanding Horizons, Rawat Publications, Jaipur and New Delhi, 2001.

Chatterjee, A. Shoma, *The Indian Women's Search for An Identity*, Vikas, New Delhi, 1988.

Chattopadhyay, K., *Indian Women's Battle for Freedom*, Abhinav Publications, New Delhi, 1983.

Chaudhary, Sukant. K., "Reflections on Emancipation of Tribal Women", *Indian Anthropologist*, Vol. 30(1-2), June-December 2000.

—, *Tribal Identity*, Rawat Publications, Jaipur and New Delhi, 2004.

Chaudhuri, Maitrayee, "Gender in the Making of the Indian Nation-State", *Sociological Bulletin*, Vol. 48(1-2), March-September 1999.

—, *Feminism in India*, Kali for Women, New Delhi, 2004.

Chekki, D.A., *Modernization and Kin Network*, Leiden: E.J. Brill, 1974.

Chitnis, Suma, "Education for Equality: Case of Schedule Caste in Higher Education", *Economic and Political Weekly*, (Special Number), 7 (31-3), 1972.

—, "The Teacher's Role in the College System", unpublished Ph.D. thesis, Tata Institute of Social Sciences, Bombay, 1973.

—, "Education as the Instrument for Social Reconstruction: The Case of the Untouchables in India", paper presented for VIII World Congress of Sociology, Toronto, 1974.

Clifford, Geertz, *Old Societies and New States: The Quest for Modernity in Asia and Africa*, New York: Free Press of Glencoe, 1963.

Cormack, Margaret L., *The Hindu Women*, Columbia University Press, 1953.

—, *She Who Rides a Peacock*, Asia Publishing House, Bombay, 1960.

Cottrell, Jr. L.S., "The Adjustment of the Individual to his Age and Sex Roles", *American Sociological Review*, 4, 1942.

Dasgupta, Susmita, "Newness and Respect for Academic Tradition in Indian Sociology", *Sociological Bulletin*, Vol. 47(2), September 1998.

Deautsch, Karl W., "Social Mobilization and Political Development", *American Political Science Review*, Vol. LV, No. 3, 1961.

Desai, A.R., *Essays on Modernization of Underdeveloped Societies*, (ed.), Thacker, 2V, Bombay, 1971.

Desai, Neera, *Women in Modern India*, Vohra and Company Publishers Pvt. Ltd., 1962.

—, *Women in Modern India*, Vohra and Company Publishers Pvt. Ltd., Bombay, 1977.

Desai, Neera and Anantram, "Review of Studies in Middle Class Women's Entry into the World of Work", *Golden Jubilee Symposium*, Vol. I, 1985.

Desai, Neera and Patel, *Indian Women: Change and Challenges in the International Decade 1975-1985*, Popular Prakashan, Bombay, 1985.

Devi, Lalitha U., *Status and Employment of Women in India*, B.R. Publishing Corporation, 1982.

Diamant, Alfred, *Political Development: Approaches to Development: Politics, Administration and Change*, (eds.), John D. Montgomery and William J. Siffins, McGraw Hill Book Co., New York, 1966.

Dobzhansky, Thedosius, *Mankind Evolving: The Evolution of the Human Species*, New Haven: Yale University Press, 1963.

Dube, S.C., "Men and Women's Role in India", in *Women in New Asia* (ed.) by Barbara E. Ward, UNESCO, Paris, 1963.

—, *Contemporary India and Its Modernization*, Vikas, New Delhi, 1974.

Dumont, Louis, *The Conception of Kinship in Ancient India, Contribution to Indian Sociology*, (eds.) Dumont and David Pocock, Mouton and Co., No. VI, 1962.

—, *Homo Hierarchicus*, Vikas, New Delhi, 1968.

Eisenstadt, S.N., *Modernization: Growth and Diversity*, Bloomington, Indiana: Indiana University Press, 1963.

—, "Social Change Differentiation and Evolution", *American Sociological Review*, No. 29, June, 1964.

—, "Social Transformation in Modernization", *American Sociological Review*, 30 No. 5, October, 1965.

—, "The Development of Socio-Political Conters at the Second Stage of Modernization: A Comparative Analysis of two types", *International Journal of Comparative Sociology*, Vol. VII, No. 1-2, March, 1966.

Epstein, C.F., *Women's Place*, University of California Press, Berkeley, 1970.

Everett, J.M., *Women and Social Change in India*, Heritage, New Delhi, 1979.

Fairchild, J.L., *Women, Society and Sex*, (eds.), Sheridon, New York, 1953.

Foster, G.M., *Traditional Cultures and the Impact of Technological Change*, Harper and Brothers, New York, 1962.

Getzels, J.W and E.G. Guba, Role, "Role Conflict and Effectiveness", *American Sociological Review*, 19, 1954.

Giddens, Anthony, *Consequences of Modernity*, Cambridge: Polity, 1990.

—, *Modernity and Self-Identity: Self and Society in a Late Modern Age*, Cambridge: Polity, 1992.

Goldstein, Rhoda L., *Indian Women in Transition: A Bangalore Case Study*, The Scarecrow Press, Metuchen, New Jersey, 1972.

—, "Tradition and Change in the Roles of Educated Indian Women", in *Explorations in the Family and other Essays*, (ed.) by D. Narain, Thacker and Co., Bombay, 1975.

Gore, M.S., *Urbanization and Family Change*, Popular Prakashan, Bombay, 1968.

—, *Education and Modernization in India*, Rawat Publications, Jaipur and New Delhi, 1982.

Gorwaney, N., *Self Image and Social Change: A Study of Female Students*, Sterling Publishers, New Delhi, 1977.

Government of India, *Towards Equality: Report of the Committee on the Status of Women in India*, Ministry of Education and Social Welfare, New Delhi, 1974.

Grace, G.R., *Role Conflict and Teacher*, London: Routledge and Kegan Paul, 1972.

Gullahorn, J.T., "Measuring Role Conflict", *American Journal of Sociology*, 1956.

Gupta, Dipankar, *Mistaken Modernity*, Harper Collins Publishers, India, 2000.

Gusfield, Joseph R., *Political Community and Group Interests in Modern India*, Mimeo, July, 1964.

—, "Tradition and Modernity: Misplaced Polarities in the Study of Social Change", *American Journal of Sociology*, Vol. 72, No. 4, January 1967.

Hagen, Everett E., *On the Theory of Social Change*, The Dorset Press, Honewood, Illinois, 1962.

Hall, D.T., "A Model Coping with Role Conflict: The Role Behaviour of College Educated Women", *Administrative Science Quarterly*, 17, 1972.

Hallen, G.C., "Attitudes of Educated Youth Towards Marriage", *Social Welfare*, 12(Feb.), 1966.

Hate, C.A., *Changing Status of Women in Post-Independence India*, Allied Publishers Pvt. Ltd., Bombay, 1969.

Haq, E., *Education and Political Culture in India*, Sterling Publishers, New Delhi, 1981.

Hawley, P., "Perceptions of Models of Feminity related to Career Choice", *Journal of Counselling Psychology*, 18, 1971.

Heer, D.M., "Dominance and the Working Wife", *Social Forces*, Vol. 28, No. 2, 1958.

Holt and Turner, *The Political Basis of Economic Development: An Exploration in Comparative Political Analysis*, D. Van Nostrand Co., New Jersey, 1966.

Horowitz, Irving L., *Three Worlds of Development*, Oxford University Press, New York, 1966.

Hunter, Guy, *Modernizing Peasant Societies*, Oxford University Press, New York, 1969.

Inkeles, A., "The Modernization of Man", in M. Weiner (ed.), *Modernization*, Inc. Publishers, 1966.

Jain, D., *Indian Women Today and Tomorrow*, Nehru Memorial Museum and Library, New Delhi, 1982.

Jain, S., *Muslims and Modernization*, Rawat Publications, Jaipur and New Delhi, 1986.

Jamenson, Fredric, "Post-modernism and Consumer Society", in *Post-modernism and its Discontents: Theories and Practices*, (ed.), E.A. Kaplan, New York: Verso, 1988.

Jayaswal, R.P., *Modernization and Youth in India*, Rawat Publications, Jaipur and New Delhi, 1993.

Jeffery, Roger and Basu, Alka M., *Girls' Schooling, Women's Autonomy and Fertility Change in South Asia*, Sage Publications, New Delhi, 1996.

Jethani, Urmila, *Single Women*, Rawat Publications, Jaipur and New Delhi, 1994.

Jha, B.N., *Adhunik Bharat Mein Jati Evam Siksha*, Janki Prakashan, Patna, 1985.

Jha, K.N., *Women Towards Modernization*, Janki Prakashan, Patna, 1985.

Jha, Kali Nath and Singh, Vinita, "Sexuality and the Markets: A Study of Women Migrant Workers in Ranchi", paper presented in the XXIX All India Sociological Conference, Udaipur, December 21-23, 2003.

—, "Quest for Participatory Democracy: Alienation of Women in Jharkhand", paper presented at International Seminar on Global

Quest for Participatory Democracy, JNU, New Delhi, Feb. 20-22, 2004.

—, "Women Haria Sellers: At Cross Roads", paper presented in the National Seminar on 'Tribes, State Policies and NGOs' organised by Indian Anthropological Association, New Delhi, March 26-27, 2004.

Judge, P. S. et al., (ed.), *Development, Gender and Diaspora: Context of Globalization*, Rawat Publications, Jaipur and New Delhi, 2003.

Kahene, Reuven, *The Problem of Political Legitimacy in Antagonistic society: The Indonesia Case*, Beverly Hills: Sage Publications, 1973.

Kapur, Promilla, *Marriage and the Working Women in India*, Vikas, New Delhi, 1970.

—, *Love, Marriage and Sex*, Vikas, New Delhi, 1973.

—, *The Changing Status of the Working Women in India*, Vikas, New Delhi, 1974.

—, "Studies on Urban Women in India", in *Family and Social Change in Modern India*, (ed.), Giriraj Gupta, Main Currents in Indian Sociology–II, Vikas, New Delhi, 1976.

—, *Empowering The Indian Women*, Publication Division, Government of India, New Delhi, 2001.

Kara, M., *Impact of Industrialization on Women*, Janta, Vol. 26, No. 1-3, 1971.

Kearney, Robert N., *Politics and Modernization in South and Southeast Asia*, John Wiley and Sons, New York, 1975.

Khanna, G. and Varghese, *Indian Women Today*, Vikas, New Delhi, 1978.

Kothari, R., *Caste in Indian Politics*, Orient Longman, New Delhi, 1970(a).

—, *Politics in India*, Orient Longman, New Delhi, 1970(b).

Kumar, Vivek, "Globalization and Empowerment of Dalits in India", *Indian Anthropologist*, Vol. 31(2), December 2001.

Kuthiala, S.K., *From Tradition to Modernity*, Abhinav Prakashan, New Delhi, 1973.

Lerner, Daniel, *The Passing of Traditional Society: Modernizing the Middle East*, The Free Press, New York, 1966.

Lerner, Daniel and Wibur Schramm, *Communication and Change in the Developing Countries*, (eds.), Honolulu East Centre Press, 1967.

Levy, M.J., *Modernization and the Structure of Societies*, Vol. I & II, Princeton: Princeton University Press, 1966.

Levy, M.J. Jr., *Contrasting Factors in the Modernization of China and Japan*, (eds.), Simon Kuznets, Wilbert E Moore and Joseph J. Spengler, Duke University Press, Durhun, N.C., 1955.

Loomis, C.P. and Beegle, J.A., *Rural Social System*, New York: Prentice Hall, Inc., 1951.

Mahajani, Usha, "Women's Status and Modernization in Southeast Asia: The Philippines Model", in *Women of the World* (eds.), by Urmilla Phadnis and Indira Malani, Vikas, New Delhi, 1978.

Malhautra, M., *New Century: Whose Century?* (ed.), UBSPD. 2001.

Mann, Michel, *Sociology*, Macmillan Press, London, 1983.

Manorama Bai, H., "Educated Women: Marriage or Career", *Social Welfare*, Vol. 13, 1966.

Mathew, A., "Expectations of College Students regarding their Marriage", *Journal of Family Welfare*, 12 (March) 1966.

Mathur, D., *Women, Family and Work*, Rawat Publications, Jaipur and New Delhi, 1993.

Mathur, S.S., *A Sociological Approach to Indian Education*, Vinod Pustak Mandir, Agra, 1997.

McClelland, David C., *The Achieving Society*, N.J.: Van Nostrand, Princeton, 1961.

Mehta, Rama, *The Western Educated Hindu Women*, Asia Publishing House, Bombay, 1970.

—, *Divorced Hindu Women*, Vikas, New Delhi, 1975.

Mehta, V., *Attitude of Educated Women towards Social Issues*, National, New Delhi, 1979.

Merchant, K.T., *Changing Views on Marriage and the Family*, B.G. Paul and Co., Madras, 1953.

Mies, M., *Indian Women and Patriarchy: Conflicts and Dilemmas of Students and Working Women*, Concept Publishing House, New Delhi, 1980.

Mishra, Saraswati, *Status of Indian Women*, Gyan Publishing House, New Delhi, 2002.

Mehrotra, Nilika, "Grassroots Women Activism: A Case Study from Delhi", *Indian Anthropologist*, Vol. 27 (2), December 1997.

—, "Understanding Feminism in a Local Context", *Indian Anthropologist*, Vol. 31(1), June-December 2001.

—, "Perceiving Feminism: Some Local Responses", *Sociological Bulletin*, Vol. 51(1), March 2002.

Mulay, Sumati and Ray, G.L., *Towards Modernization*, National, Delhi, 1973.

Myrdal, Gunnar, *Asian Drama*, Vol. I, Pantheon, New York, 1968.

Nagla, B.K., (ed.) *Political Sociology*, Rawat Publications, Jaipur and New Delhi, 1999.

Nagla, Madhu, *Sociology of Medical Profession*, Rawat Publications, Jaipur and New Delhi, 1997.

Nett, J.P. and Robertson, *International System and Modernization of Societies*, Basic Books, Inc., New York, 1968.

Newcomb, T.M., *Social Psychology*, The Dryden Press, New York, 1950.

Nye, I.F. and Hoffman, *The Employed Mothers in America*, Rand McNally and Co., Chicago, 1963.

Pandey, S., *Women in Politics*, Rawat Publications, Jaipur, 1990.

Panini, M.N., "Trends in Cultural Globalization: From Agriculture to Agribusiness in Karnataka", *Economic and Political Weekly*, July 31, 1999.

Pannikar, K.M., *Hindu Society at the Cross Roads*, Asia Publishers, New Delhi, 1961.

Parsons, T., *The Structure of Social Action*, The Free Press of Glencoe, 1961.

—, "Evolutionary Universals in Society", *American Sociological Review*, Vol. 29, No. 3, 1964.

Patel, Vibhuti, *Women's Challenges of the New Millennium*, Gyan Publishing House, New Delhi, 2002.

Prasad, P.H., "Caste and Class in Bihar", *Economic and Political Weekly*, XV (5, 6 and 7), 1979.

Pundir, J.K., *Changing Patterns of Scheduled Castes*, Rawat Publications, Jaipur and New Delhi, 1997.

Pye, Lucian, *Politics, Personality and Nation-building: Burma's Search for Identity*, Yale University Press, New Haven, 1963.

Pye, Lucian and Verba, *Political Culture and Political Development*, Princeton University Press, New Jersey, 1965.

Rande, S.N. and Ramchandran, *Women and Employment*, Tata Institute of Social Sciences, Bombay, 1970.

Rani, Kala, *Role Conflict in Working Women*, Chetna Publications, New Delhi, 1976.

Ranjan, Kumud, *Women and Modern Occupation in India*, Chug Publications, Allahabad, 1993.

Rawls, A., *Theory of Justice*, Cambridge, Massachusetts: The Belknep Press of Harvard University, 1971.

Robertson, R., "Globalization or Glocalization?" *Journal of International Communication*, Vol. 1, No. 1, 1994.

Rudolph and Rudolph, *The Modernity of Tradition: Political Development in India*, Chicago University Press, Chicago, 1967.

Rostow, W.W., *Stages of Economic Growth*, Cambridge University Press, New York, 1960.

Sahay, Gaurang R., "Caste and Agrarian Economic Structure: A Study of Rural Bihar", *Sociological Bulletin*, Vol. 51(2), September 2002.

—, "Hierarchy, Difference and the Caste System: A Study of Rural Bihar", *Contributions to Indian Sociology*, Vol. 38(1-2), January-August, 2004.

Sahay, Sarita, *Tribal Women in the New Profile*, Anmol Publications Pvt. Ltd., New Delhi, 2002.

Saksena, R.N., "Modernization and Development: Trends in India", *Sociological Bulletin*, 21 (2), 1970.

Sethi, R.M., *Modernization of Working Women in Developing Societies*, National Publishing House, New Delhi, 1976.

Shah, B.V., *Social Change and College Students of Gujarat*, M.S. University of Baroda, Baroda, 1964.

Sharma, K.L., "Modernization and Rural Stratification: An Application at the Micro-Level", *Economic and Political Weekly*, 5 (37), 1977.

—, *Social Stratification and Mobility*, Rawat Publications, Jaipur, (reprint), 1997.

—, *Reconceptualizing Caste Class and Tribe*, Rawat Publications, Jaipur and New Delhi, 2001.

Shils, Edward, *The Intellectual Between Tradition and Modernity: The Indian Situation*, The Hague: Mouton, 1961.

Singer, Milton, *When a Great Tradition Modernizes: An Anthropological Approach to Indian Civilization*, Vikas, New Delhi, 1972.

Singh, Indu Prakash, *Indian Women: The Captured Beings*, Intellectual Publishing House, New Delhi, 1990.

Singh, K.S., *People of India: An Introduction*, Calcutta: Anthropological Survey of India, 1992.

Singh, Vinita and Jha, Kali Nath, "Emerging Professionals: Saleswomen in Ranchi", paper presented in the XXIX All India Sociological Conference, Udaipur, December 21-23, 2003.

—, "Process of Globalization: A Study of Tribal Women Students in Ranchi", paper presented in the Golden Jubilee National Seminar on

'Anthropology and the Challenges of Development in Jharkhand', organised by Department of Anthropology, Ranchi University, Ranchi and Anthropological Survey of India, New Delhi, January 19-21, 2004.

—, "Migration of Tribal Women from Jharkhand: The Price of Development", paper presented in the National Seminar on 'Tribes, State Policies and NGOs, organised by Indian Anthropological Association, New Delhi, March 26-27, 2004.

Singh, Yogendra, "Cultural Integration and Changing Values (A Study of Value System of Educated Youth)", *Sociological Bulletin*, Vol. XIII, 1964.

—, "Caste and Class: Some Aspects of Continuity and Change", *Sociological Bulletin*, 1968.

—, *Modernization of Indian Tradition: A Systematic Study of Social Change*, (Reprint), Rawat Publications, Jaipur, 1988.

—, *Social Stratification and Change in India*, Manohar, New Delhi, 1977.

—, *Essays on Modernization in India*, Manohar, New Delhi, 1978.

—, *Images of Man: Ideology and Theory in Indian Sociology*, Chanakya, New Delhi, 1984.

—, *Indian Sociology: Social Conditioning and Emerging Concerns*, Vistaar Publications, New Delhi, 1986.

—, *Social Change in India: Crisis and Resistance*, Haranand, New Delhi, 1993.

—, "The Desired Role of Political Leadership in Economic Reforms", in *Indian Economy and the Institutional Set-up*, in J.L. Bajaj (ed.) Delhi: Policy Group, 1999.

—, *Culture Change in India: Identity and Globalization*, Rawat Publications, Jaipur and New Delhi, 2000.

—, *Ideology and Theory in Indian Sociology*, Rawat Publications, Jaipur and New Delhi, 2004.

Sinha, Puspa, *Role Conflict Among the Working Women*, Janki Prakashan, Patna, 1986.

Sood, Rita, *Changing Status and Adjustment of Women*, Manak Publications Pvt. Ltd., Delhi and Jaipur, 1991.

Srinivas, M.N., *Social Change in Modern India*, Berkeley: California University Press, 1966.

—, *Changing Status of Indian Women*, Oxford University Press, London, 1978.

Suguna, B., *Working Women and Religion*, Discovery Publishing House, 1994.

Sujatha, V., *Health by the People: Sociology of Medical Lore*, Rawat Publications, Jaipur and New Delhi, 2003.

Tachau, Frank, *The Developing Nations: What Path to Modernization?* Dodd, Mead and Co., New York, 1972.

Tangri, Shanti S., "Intellectuals and Society in Nineteenth-Century India", *Comparative Studies and History*, Vol. 3, 1960-61.

Tilly, C., "Does Modernization Breed Revolution?" *Comparative Politics*, 5, 1973.

Touraine, Alain, *Critique of Modernity*, Oxford: Blackwell, 1995.

Toynbee, A.J., *A Study of History*, Vol. 8, Oxford University Press, London, 1963.

Tripathy, H., "Changing Attitude of Women in Post-Independent India", *Journal of Gujarat Research Society*, XIXX (2/114), 1967.

Vajpeyi, D.K., *Modernization and Social Change in India*, Manohar, New Delhi, 1979.

Vidyarthi, L.P., *Socio-Culture Implications of Industrialization in India: Case Study of Tribal Bihar*, Ranchi University, Ranchi, 1970.

Weiner, Myron, *The Politics of Scarcity*, Chicago University Press, Chicago, 1962.

—, *Modernization: The Dynamics of Growth*, Basic Books, New York, 1966.

Weintraub, D., *Development and Modernization in the Philippines: The Problem of Change in the Context of Political Stability and Social Continuity*, Sage Publications, Beverly Hills, 1973.

Wertheim, W.F., *East-West Parallels*, The Hague: W. Van Hague Ltd., 1968.

Whiting, Gordon C., "Empathy, Mass Media and Modernization: A Study of Rural Brazil", Ph.D. Thesis, Michigan State University, 1967.

Zovorikine, A.A., "Some Problems of the Theory of Culture", *Socialist Digest*, No. 2, June, 1968.

Index